W9-BSO-142

· ART MAKERS ·

EMPOWERED EMBROIDERY

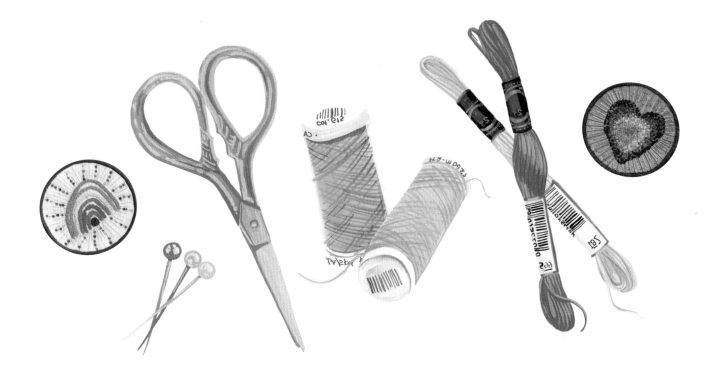

Amy L. Frazer

Brimming with creative inspiration, how-to projects, and useful information to enrich your everyday life, Quarto Knows is a favorite destination for those pursuing their interests and passions. Visit our site and dig deeper with our books into your area of interest: Quarto Creates, Quarto Cooks, Quarto Homes, Quarto Lives, Quarto Drives, Quarto Explores, Quarto Gifts, or Quarto Kids.

© 2021 Quarto Publishing Group USA Inc.
Artwork and text © 2021 Amy L. Frazer. Photos on pages 51, 65, 81, 95, 111, and 125 © Kayley Hoddick, Hoddick Photography. Photos on pages 127 and 128 © Gia Goodrich.

First published in 2021 by Walter Foster Publishing, an imprint of The Quarto Group.
26391 Crown Valley Parkway, Suite 220, Mission Viejo, CA 92691, USA.
T (949) 380-7510 F (949) 380-7575 **www.QuartoKnows.com**

All rights reserved. No part of this book may be reproduced in any form without written permission of the copyright owners. All images in this book have been reproduced with the knowledge and prior consent of the artists concerned, and no responsibility is accepted by producer, publisher, or printer for any infringement of copyright or otherwise, arising from the contents of this publication. Every effort has been made to ensure that credits accurately comply with information supplied. We apologize for any inaccuracies that may have occurred and will resolve inaccurate or missing information in a subsequent reprinting of the book.

Walter Foster Publishing titles are also available at discount for retail, wholesale, promotional, and bulk purchase. For details, contact the Special Sales Manager by email at specialsales@quarto.com or by mail at The Quarto Group, Attn: Special Sales Manager, 100 Cummings Center, Suite 265D, Beverly, MA 01915, USA.

ISBN: 978-1-63322-884-9

Digital edition published in 2021
eISBN: 978-1-63322-885-6

Printed in China
10 9 8 7 6 5 4 3 2 1

R0459508465

TABLE OF CONTENTS

Introduction 4

Essential Tools & Materials 6

Drawing Ideas 12

Getting Started 18

Stitching Guide & Techniques 20

Stitch Map 30

Transferring Designs to Fabric 32

Step-by-Step Drawing & Embroidery Projects

    Frida Kahlo 36

    Eleanor Roosevelt 52

    Maya Angelou 66

    Harriet Tubman 82

    Ruth Bader Ginsburg 96

    Michelle Obama 112

Resources 126

About the Artist 128

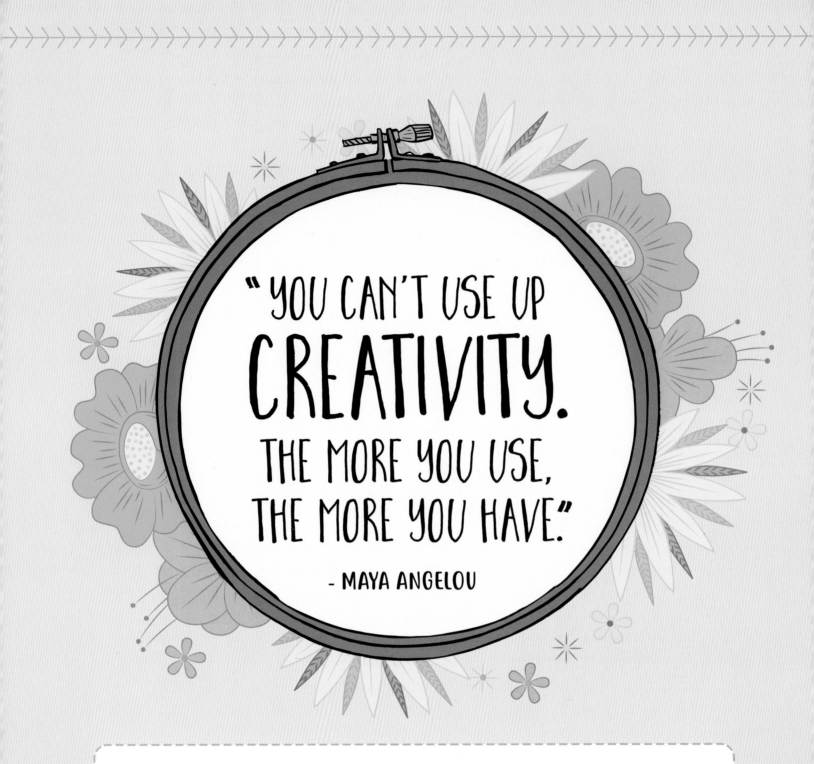

"YOU CAN'T USE UP CREATIVITY. THE MORE YOU USE, THE MORE YOU HAVE."

- MAYA ANGELOU

Introduction

As I wrote, illustrated, and embroidered the artwork in this book during the worldwide COVID-19 pandemic of 2020, I spent hours upon hours in my studio and often listened to podcasts and audiobooks such as Michelle Obama's *Becoming*, Maya Angelou's *I Know Why the Caged Bird Sings*, and Ruth Bader Ginsburg's *My Own Words*. Listening to the stories of these courageous women, often in their own voices, helped me to stay present in my work. Learning more about their tragedies and triumphs helped me focus and brought me back to the present moment. I was inspired as I researched and designed each project, sorting through and organizing my threads, fabrics, and beads.

A few years ago, I got a sleeve tattooed on my arm that depicts the birth month flowers of myself, my mom, and my granny. In this way, I connected our lives through art and flowers. Consider how your life and experiences can be connected to the people you admire and use that inspiration as a meditation as you stitch. Think about embroidery as a way to do justice to these women and honor their lifetimes of work that are paving the way for future generations.

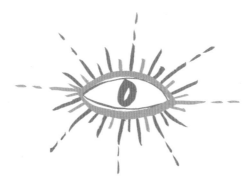

This book is about more than just drawing and stitching portraits. I want to encourage you to find people that inspire you from all walks of life, races, and religions. Maybe you're inspired by your grandmother who was born in a time when women did not yet have the right to vote, or a Swedish teenager fighting to save our planet. Sources of inspiration are everywhere around us, and telling these women's stories through stitching is a way to honor their work and keep their messages of hope, activism, leadership, community building, and persistence alive.

I hope this book will inspire you to research people from your past and present, so you may discover and tell their stories. Use art and embroidery to document their lives, whether you embroider a quote, a favorite flower, or a full portrait. And remember that capturing someone's exact likeness isn't necessarily the goal here. The objective is to capture what these women mean to you—their energy and inspiration—and to interpret that into art and embroidery.

ESSENTIAL TOOLS 3 MATERIALS

When I was a kid growing up in Ohio, my favorite time of year was back to school. Because I wore a uniform, I didn't get a lot of new school clothes, so my focus became my supplies. After we went to the store, supply list in hand, my mom stashed my supplies in her closet. I would often sneak in there and reorganize the pencils, folders, and glue sticks, waiting for the first day of school when I could put them to good use. To this day, I'm obsessed with art materials and office supplies.

As with any hobby, craft, or art practice, you will acquire all kinds of sewing notions (supplies). Start out with the basics and build your collection of supplies as you continue your stitching journey.

In this chapter, I'll walk you through the basic toolkit you'll need as we work through the projects in this book. I encourage you to experiment and discover what types of fabric you prefer, which needles become your go-tos, and the perfect sewing snips (mine are my granny's little gold ones). For information on where to find drawing and embroidery supplies and which items I use in my art, see "Resources" on pages 126-127.

In My Toolbox

FABRIC

If you're like me, you probably have a nice stash of fabrics in all sorts of colors, textures, and patterns. We collect them along the way, saved from worn-out clothing, bandannas, friends' unwanted items, vintage fabrics, and so on.

For most of the projects in this book, however, I've chosen to use solid-color woven fabrics like linen and cotton. I generally wash store-bought fabrics by hand or in the washing machine on the delicate cycle and line dry to preshrink it.

The most important thing to consider when choosing a base fabric is the relationship between your fabric and threads, and to think about what your final embroidery will be used for. Using a thicker thread or yarn calls for a more open-weave fabric, while thinner threads can be used on tighter weaves. Test out the fabric, needle, and thread combination to make sure it glides through the fabric without getting stuck, and that you like the effect.

PLAIN-WEAVE FABRIC

Fabrics that are best suited for embroidery, such as cotton and linen, are called "plain weave." This means that the warp and weft, or threads that run horizontally and vertically, are irregular and don't require you to pay particular attention to where your needle enters the fabric. These are the fabrics that I will be using for projects in this book.

Some examples of fabrics that I love to use are:

- 100-percent quilting-weight cotton: The most common cotton-weight fabric, it can be found in craft and fabric stores in a range of weights, colors, and prints.

- Linen or linen blends: My absolute favorite type of fabric to stitch on is linen. The weight is perfect for hand stitching and it comes in a variety of colors and blends such as linen/rayon or linen/cotton.

- Felt: One of my other favorite materials to stitch on, it comes in a wide variety of colors, and unlike woven fabrics, the edges won't fray when cut. You can get wool felt, acrylic, or wool blends.

As a general rule, woven fabrics work better for embroidery than knits, due to their stability. Knits can certainly be worked with, but due to their stretchiness, they can change shape pretty dramatically when taken out of the hoop.

TIP

A great way to freshen up an older piece of clothing, like a cotton top or a jean jacket, is to embroider on it. You'll breathe new life into the clothing and have a one-of-a-kind piece to show off!

NEEDLES

The thickness of your needle should match the thickness of your thread. Pick a needle that's too big for your thread and you'll leave holes in the fabric. Pick a needle that's too small, and the thread won't be able to pass through the eye. Experiment with different sizes of threads and needles to find what works best for you. I usually sew with three strands of floss and a size five embroidery needle or a 22 or 24 chenille needle. You'll want a needle with a bigger eye if you use more strands of floss.

It's helpful to have a needle book or a piece of felt to keep your needles in one place. It's also a real time saver to load up several needles with thread and put them in your needle book so that they are ready to go for a project.

  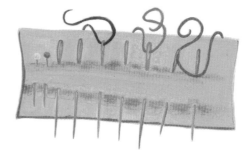

TYPES OF NEEDLES

- Embroidery (crewel): Medium length with sharp points and relatively large eyes, these are used for most hand stitching. They are sized in reverse order, so the larger the number, the finer the needle.

- Chenille: Longer and thicker than embroidery needles, these have a large eye and sharp point. Chenille needles are useful for thicker threads, ribbon, or yarn.

- Tapestry: These needles have a blunt point and large eyes and are great for counted embroidery work like cross stitch. They won't pierce the threads of your fabric; instead, they slip between threads without splitting.

- Milliners (or straw): These are long, sharp needles traditionally used in the millinery trade that are great for making French knots and long bullion knots. The eye and the shaft of the needle are the same size all the way up, which means that the needle will slip more easily through wraps.

- Beading needles: Very long and thin needles made especially for beading.

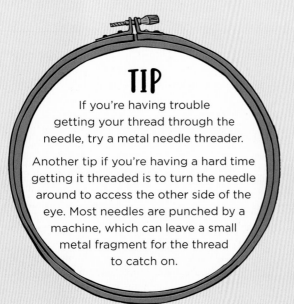

TIP

If you're having trouble getting your thread through the needle, try a metal needle threader.

Another tip if you're having a hard time getting it threaded is to turn the needle around to access the other side of the eye. Most needles are punched by a machine, which can leave a small metal fragment for the thread to catch on.

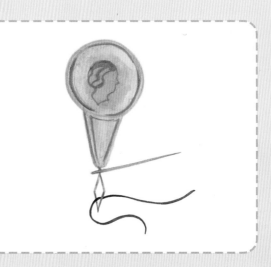

THREADS

There are so many different types of threads and yarns. For me, if it fits through the eye of a needle, I'll embroider with it. Try varying the weight of the threads to create different textures in your embroidery. A single strand of sewing thread will create a very different look than a wool yarn. Practice making the same stitch using different types of thread or yarn as a fun exercise. This is modern embroidery and there are not a lot of rules here!

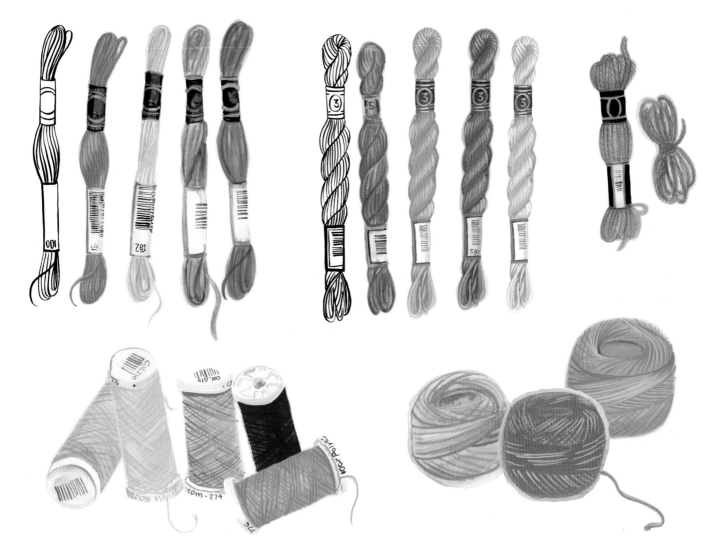

TYPES OF THREADS

- Cotton embroidery floss: DMC® six-strand cotton floss is the most commonly used embroidery thread and one that I use all the time. It's easy to find at your local craft or fabric store and comes in a wide array of colors. This thread is made up of six strands twisted together and can be separated, allowing you to modify the thickness of the floss depending on the number of strands you use.

- Perle cotton: Unlike embroidery floss, this cannot be separated. It is a mercerized, twisted single strand and comes in a range of colors and thicknesses. It has a beautiful sheen and is soft to sew with.

- Sewing thread: Use this for machine and hand stitching. It comes in a huge array of colors and fibers including cotton, polyester, rayon, and silk. It's great for fine lines and details.

- Metallic perle and metallic sewing thread: Metallic threads come in a limited number of colors and are great for adding highlights, although they are sometimes difficult to work with and require patience. It's best to use shorter lengths of metallic threads (12 inches) and either one or two strands at a time.

- Crewel yarn: A fine, two-ply thread (two strands twisted to make one) that's usually wool. Several strands can be combined to make a thicker line.

SCISSORS

Having the right scissors on hand for embroidering will make life so much easier for you! Keep them sharp and use them for their intended purpose. It can be difficult to snip thin threads with scissors that are too large. I have a few pairs of my grandmother's scissors that don't leave my studio, as well as a few other pairs that I can travel with in case they get lost.

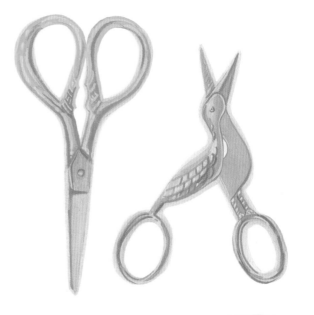

- Embroidery scissors: It's important to have a small pair of sharp scissors to cut threads with. I use the kind with a curve on the tip to help get under small stitches. It's important to keep these special scissors only for cutting threads; don't use them for paper, fabric, or anything else!

- Fabric shears: These shears have long, sharp blades and are used to cut the fabric you'll embroider on. Don't use them for paper or plastic, as they will get dull faster. As an alternative, I often use a rotary cutter and a metal straight edge to cut my fabric.

- Regular all-purpose scissors: These are great for cutting paper and water-soluble stabilizer (see page 33).

- Pinking shears: Nice to have but not necessary, these cut a zigzag line and help prevent fabric from fraying when cut. They are great for creating a decorative edge on felt.

- Seam ripper and tweezers: While technically not scissors, these tools are handy if you need to unpick stitches. For densely stitched areas, try snipping the threads with embroidery scissors and gently pulling them out with tweezers. Tweezers are also great to use when working with beads.

HOOPS & FRAMES

To hoop or not to hoop? That is the question. I personally almost always use a hoop. I like to keep my fabric flat and tight when stitching. If I'm stitching something larger like the portraits in this book, I prefer to use a larger hoop or frame so that I can see most of the embroidery all at once. If you use water-soluble stabilizer to transfer your designs to fabric, I suggest using a hoop.

VINTAGE METAL HOOP

- Wooden or plastic hoop: Hoops come in a wide range of sizes, from about 3 to 14 inches or larger. Quilting hoops are even bigger. A quality hoop will maintain the fabric at an even tension and keep the grain straight. This will allow you to keep the stitches even and consistent. If the hoop seems loose, you can wrap the inner ring with a long ¼-inch strip of fabric to keep it nice and tight.

- Plastic square frame: These come in a variety of sizes and have pieces that snap together. They are great for working on larger projects and keeping your fabric taut, and I like them because my work is often square or rectangular and fits in the frame perfectly.

- Floor or table stand: These are helpful if you are using a larger hoop or just want to free up your hands so you don't have to hold the hoop. Totally optional, but nice to have!

WOODEN HOOP

Other Embroidery & Sewing Supplies

These sewing supplies are nice to have but not totally necessary to get started. I will discuss other materials specific to drawing and transferring images in later chapters.

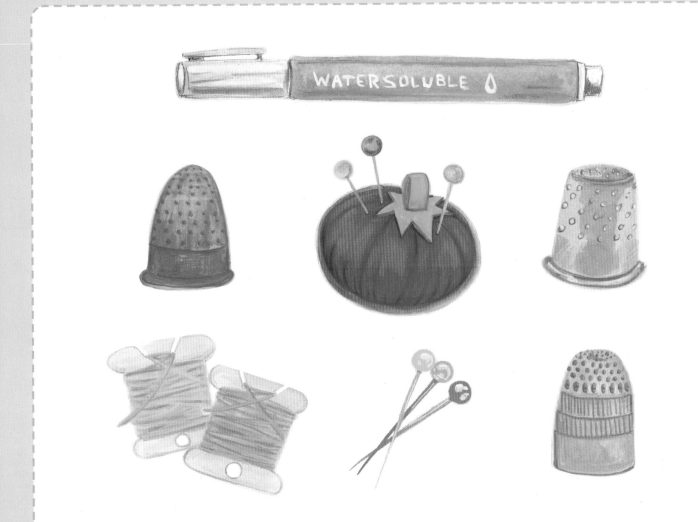

- Storage container: I like to keep the threads and materials I use for each project in a small box so that I can just pull it out when I want to work on a certain piece.

- Thimbles: I don't use thimbles that often, but they are great to have in case you need to push your needle through a thick patch of stitches or a few layers of fabric. I like to collect a few different kinds like metal, rubber, and decorative ones—just for fun.

- Floss bobbins: Either plastic or cardboard, these work well for keeping your thread organized.

- Iron and ironing surface

- Thread conditioner: You can swipe the end of your thread through this to help thread the needle, or you can pull your full length of thread through it to put a protective layer on the thread.

- Needle threader

- Quilting pins: When I'm using a large piece of water-soluble stabilizer, it's sometimes helpful to pin it down in a few spots to keep it from shifting around.

- Water-soluble pens or pencils

DRAWING IDEAS

For me, designing an embroidery is equal parts research project and drawing assignment. Let me explain. Before I pick up a pencil to start sketching, I research the subject to gain inspiration.

I'll use Frida Kahlo as an example. A few years ago, I was fortunate enough to visit her Mexico City home, where you could pay a fee to take photos. I opted not to take photos that day, which was very uncharacteristic of me! Instead, I wanted to experience the house, sights, and sounds. I have memories of her studio; the way her pigment jars and brushes were arranged on her desk; the specially made bed that she could lay in and paint from because her back was injured; and the textiles, objects, and artifacts that were once a part of her life. At that time, I had no idea that I would be writing this book that features a project dedicated to Frida. If I had known, I probably would have taken the photos!

In this chapter, I will walk you through my process of designing an embroidery, from researching and brainstorming to refining drawings before preparing them for embroidery. This is not a drawing tutorial but a lesson in turning ideas into images. I want you to understand the process of thinking about and building the stories behind the images. As you start sketching more, you'll gain the confidence to add your own ideas to my designs, eventually designing your own projects.

Inspiration & Research

To research Frida's life a bit more, adding to my memories of visiting her home, I did an online search for images of her, her home, and her incredible paintings. When possible, try to do hands-on research as well, perhaps going to a botanical garden to look at flowers and plants or taking your sketchbook to a museum. Documentaries, podcasts, and movies tell the stories of the lives of women we admire. Pinterest is a great online image-sharing platform that you can use to make digital inspiration boards, as I did for Frida.

By doing a bit of research, you will gather information and inspiration to feed your brainstorm and sketching activities.

SUGGESTIONS FOR RESEARCH

- Online search for images and articles
- Personal memories
- Quotes
- Libraries and museums
- Documentaries, movies, and podcasts

Brainstorm & Make Lists

After gathering my inspirational research, I like to make lists of words and mind maps. A mind map is a fun way to brainstorm ideas organically without too much structure. It's a way to arrange concepts, words, and thoughts linked to each other around a central concept or subject. The maps can be a simple web of connected circles, or they can be creative and colorful and incorporate simple sketches and symbols.

Sketch

This is when I begin to put my ideas on paper by sketching my thoughts and ideas into icons and images. I bring my ideas to life and give them a visual vocabulary. When referencing photographs or online images, be sure to use them as a guide, and don't copy them. Interpret and expand upon what you see, adding your own details.

I like to sketch my ideas in a sketchbook or on plain copy paper with a soft graphite pencil or brush pen. These are both great for staying loose and not getting too precise or detailed. The objective at this stage is to work quickly and connect ideas to each other when possible. How do the words and ideas translate into icons and images? What do your ideas look like?

Just know that as you sketch and ideate more, your skills will evolve and improve. Start with simple line drawings and you can continue to add more details as your drawing skills increase.

Here are a few examples of the many sketches I made for Frida Kahlo.

Refine

Now you want to consider how big or small your embroidery project will be, keeping in mind whether you will eventually frame the piece, make it into a pillow, sew it onto a tote bag, or make it into a square to be sewn into a quilt.

This is the time to decide what sketches and ideas stay and which ones get set aside for another project or kept in your sketchbook. Style and composition come into play here, and your style may be more realistic or simplistic. Think about how you want your embroidery to look. Does it consist of outlines, or are there areas that are filled with stitches to give the embroidery a bold look?

I knew for my Frida embroidery that I wanted a classic image of her facing the viewer directly and wearing a floral headband. From there, I added flowers and other symbols that I pulled from quotes and her paintings. Adding textures or flowers is a great way to fill a space with interest.

Here are some refined sketches that I did. I incorporated color and textures that will influence my thread choices.

Combine ideas and sketches and think about composition.

Start to incorporate color and textures that will influence thread choices.

Line Drawing

To make an image suitable for embroidery, it's important to transform your sketches and doodles into a clean line drawing. I use a pencil, an eraser, and tracing paper to refine my drawing and finalize the layout and details. Now that you've gone through the process from research and brainstorm to sketches and refinement of a final line drawing, focus on the essential lines needed to embroider.

Once I have my drawing finalized on tracing paper, I can then trace over that drawing using a thin-line pen. As soon you have your image in line-art format, you are ready to transfer it to fabric and can make any necessary adjustments in size.

I scanned the black-and-white images in each project in this book into my computer and then traced them into vector format using Adobe Illustrator®. This gives the lines a very clean appearance and the image can be enlarged or reduced, colored, and printed very easily. If you are making an embroidery project for your own use, there is probably no need to go to this step.

Now you can transfer your line drawing onto fabric using your chosen method (see "Transferring Designs to Fabric" on pages 32-35). This is when I usually start the process of choosing which stitches and colors of thread to use and often make a copy of my pattern and write notes on it. It's helpful to start embroidering with a plan and then adjust as you go. You are going to have so much fun when you start to customize projects and eventually start designing your own patterns!

For complete instructions for embroidering your own portrait of Frida Kahlo, see pages 36-51.

I use a pencil, an eraser, and tracing paper to refine my drawing and finalize the layout and details.

The final inked drawing being prepped for transfer.

Final vector image.

GETTING STARTED

Before you start each project, you'll need to get a couple of things ready. First, plan your project, including picking your fabric and threads, deciding on the size of the portrait, and adding or changing any elements from your sketch before transferring to the fabric. I prefer to use a hoop when stitching, as it holds my fabric flat and makes it easier to work with my needle and thread.

The base fabric should be larger than your hoop, with plenty of room around the sides of the image. You may want to frame your piece later or stitch it into a quilt, so that is something to consider now. I like to use a lightweight piece of fabric behind my base fabric, especially if it is light in color or weight. Experiment and see if you like this method too.

I like to gather my materials for each project—including threads, needles, scissors, thread conditioner, practice hoop, and pens—into a small box or pouch so that I have them at the ready when I need them.

By taking some time before beginning each project to consider and gather your materials and methods of approach, you will begin to form a creative process that works for you and that you can return to each time you embroider. Once this routine is established, your mind and hands are free to have fun with the embroidery and to play with your stitches and color.

Assembling the Embroidery Hoop

Depending on the type of hoop you are using, this process may be slightly different each time. For larger projects like portraits, I like to use a square, plastic, snap-together frame or a very large wooden hoop so that I can see the entire embroidery come together and work on different sections without moving the fabric around. If using a wooden hoop, it's helpful to bind the inner ring with a ¼- to ½-inch length of fabric strip or narrow cotton tape and to stitch or glue the two ends down. This prevents the fabric from slipping around and loosening in the hoop.

To assemble an embroidery hoop with fabric, loosen the screw of the outer ring so that it fit loosely over the inner ring. Remove the outer ring from the inner one and set aside.

After transferring the design to your fabric, center the fabric over the inner ring. If you are using a backing fabric, place this in the hoop as well. Then place the outer ring over the fabric and push the ring over the fabric, fitting it snugly onto the inner ring. Tighten the screw to hold the frame together.

Go around the edges, gently pulling the fabric snug. You will probably need to tighten the screw again. Repeat as needed.

Thread & Needle Prep

A crucial part of the creative process is preparing your tools. Pick out a few needles that you want to use for your project. You may need a couple for thicker threads, a milliners needle for French knots, and smaller ones for thinner threads. I like to load up a few needles with the colors I'm using and place them in a small piece of felt. This saves me some time when stitching.

- To start, cut about 18 inches of thread.

- Cut the end of the thread so that there are no frayed ends. Gently push the thread through the eye of the needle, using a needle threader if it's helpful.

- Some embroiderers knot their threads, while others don't. I usually start and end my stitching with a knot. You don't want the thread to pull all the way through the fabric. If you don't knot the end, you can weave the end of the thread through a few stitches.

Starting & Finishing

- With the threaded needle, bring the tip through the back of the fabric at the starting point. This is referred to as "up 1." The next step, unless you're making a knot, is "down 2." Insert the needle into the fabric and push it through, pulling the thread until it catches on the front. Continue stitching.

- As you stitch, the thread will inevitably become knotted. Don't worry! Try to unknot it, and if after a few tries, it isn't working, tie it off on the back and start with a freshly threaded needle.

- To finish stitching or to change colors, tie a small knot on the back side, close to the fabric. Run the thread under a few stitches before snipping it. Make sure that when you end a thread, you have enough length to finish it off—generally about 5 to 6 inches.

- When you finish the embroidery, look at the back side and trim and loose threads to clean up.

Sewing vs. Stabbing

For most stitches, you can either use a stabbing method or a sewing method. As you practice and learn each stitch, you will find what works best for you. I generally prefer the stabbing method because I feel I have better control over the shape, size and spacing of my stitches.

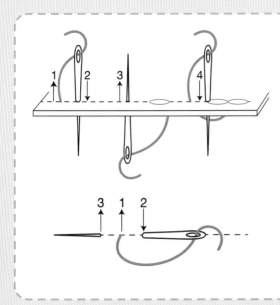

STABBING METHOD

When using the stabbing method, start by bringing the needle up through the fabric; then take the needle back down through the fabric, working the stitches in an up-and-down motion. With each stitch, the needle passes through the fabric.

SEWING METHOD

The sewing method keeps the needle above the fabric. When making a stitch, scoop under the fabric and back up in one continuous motion. Your stitching hand does all the work, and your free hand holds the hoop or fabric. Ideally your stitching hand does not go under the fabric or hoop.

STITCHING GUIDE & TECHNIQUES

Keep a Practice Hoop Handy

When I'm stitching a project, I like to keep a small hoop handy with the same base fabric I'm using for my final embroidery. I can test out stitches and colors to see how they look on the fabric color. It's also an opportunity to get messy, try new stitches, or practice stitches you haven't used in a while.

TIP

Keep a roll or length of fabric going as a daily stitching project. It's portable and easy to take almost anywhere when you have a few moments to practice. Over time, you will begin to see the progress you've made as your skills improve. You may even discover new stitch combinations to keep in your toolbox!

Stitch legend

BS=backstitch

CH=couching

CS=chain stitch

DCS=detached chain stitch

FLY=fly stitch

FK=French knot

OFB=open fish bone

RUN=running stitch

SAT=satin stitch

STR=star stitch

STM=stem stitch

SS=straight stitch

TBS=threaded backstitch

TRS=threaded running stitch

WBS=whipped backstitch

WRS=whipped running stitch

Stitches

Stitches can be divided into categories like line or straight stitches, fill stitches, long stitches, cross stitches, knotted stitches, and so on. There are hundreds of stitches and stitch combinations to explore, so I've detailed some basic stitches and variations to help get you started. When deciding what stitches to use for different areas of your embroidery, think about the effect you want to convey. Do you want to simply outline the image or make a bolder statement and fill it in?

Backstitch

The backstitch is a great stitch for outlining just about anything straight or curvy, including lettering and type. Make longer or shorter stitches for more variety.

HOW TO

Bring the needle up from the back of the fabric at 1, down at 2, back up at 3. Go back down at 4, in the same hole as step 1. The stitches form a continuous line with no breaks between them. Each stitch should be uniform in length; this will take a bit of practice. Play with the lengths of your stitches for variety.

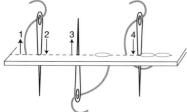

Stabbing method

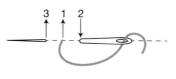

Sewing method

TIP

Draw lines on your fabric to practice stitches. Working on backstitch? Draw a straight or curvy line. You can make tick marks for the stitch length too; eventually you won't need to do this as you gain confidence.

Threaded Backstitch

This variation adds weight to the backstitch. Embroider a line of backstitches, and then starting at the beginning, bring the thread up through the stitch line and weave, or thread, in and out of the stitches. The needle does not pierce the fabric.

Whipped Backstitch

Embroider a line of backstitches. Then, starting at the beginning, bring the thread up through the stitch line, wrap the thread around the first stitch and back under the next stitch, repeating this motion as you progress down the backstitched line. The needle does not pierce the fabric.

Chain Stitch

The chain stitch is very versatile and can be used as an outline and a fill stitch, or to make little flowers. It is thicker and more textured than the backstitch and stem stitch. Play with changing stitch lengths and be sure not to pull the loop too tight or it will lose its shape.

HOW TO

Bring the needle up through the fabric from the back at 1. Form a small loop with thread, and holding the loop with your free thumb, insert the needle into the fabric in the same hole, down at 2. Bring the needle up at 3, inside the loop. As you pull it through gently, form another small loop. Insert the needle back down at 4, then up at 5, down at 6. Continue working along the design line. When the last stitch is made, finish off the loop with a short stitch to anchor it.

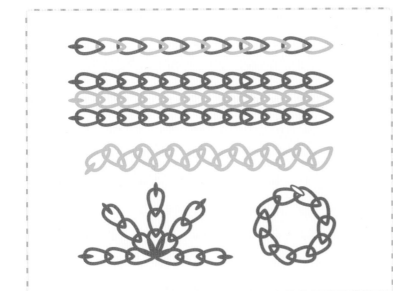

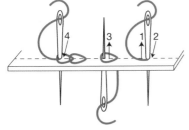

Stabbing method

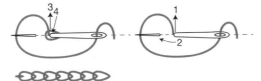

Sewing method

Detached Chain Stitch (or Lazy Daisy or Isolated Chain Stitch)

This variation on the chain stitch can be worked in singles or grouped together to form flowers and small leaves.

HOW TO

Bring the needle up through the fabric from the back at 1. Form a small loop with thread, and holding the loop with your free thumb, insert the needle into the fabric in the same hole, down at 2. Bring the needle up at 3, inside the loop. Forming a small stitch, insert the needle at 4 outside the loop. This tiny stitch will hold the loop in place.

Sewing method

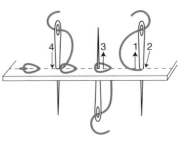

Stabbing method

Couching Stitch

The couching stitch uses two threads. The first thread is laid on the surface of the fabric and stitched down using a second thread. The laid thread is usually thicker than the sewn thread, but not always, and it can be contrasting in texture and color. You can couch with small straight stitches or other stitches, like satin or blanket stitch. Experiment with combining colors and shapes.

HOW TO

Bring your first thread up through the fabric from the back side. Lay this thread along the top of the fabric, following the design line, maneuvering it as you go. Using a second thread, stitch down the laid thread at evenly spaced intervals, going in and out of the fabric. When finished, both threads pass through to the back of the fabric and are tied off.

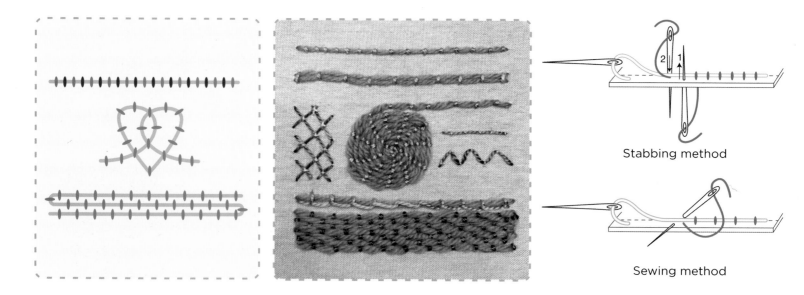

Stabbing method

Sewing method

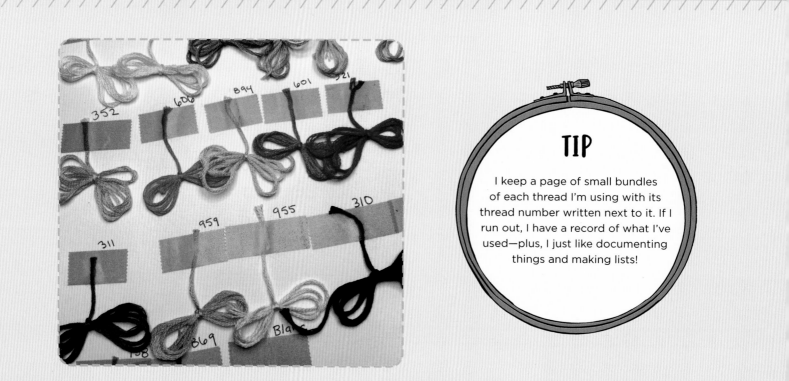

TIP

I keep a page of small bundles of each thread I'm using with its thread number written next to it. If I run out, I have a record of what I've used—plus, I just like documenting things and making lists!

French Knot

Whenever I teach workshops, everyone wants to learn how to make French knots. I totally get it! Although there is a bit of a learning curve, they are really fun and easy to make. French knots are great for filling areas, like flower centers, and adding cute random details. For me, making a French knot is all about managing the thread so that it doesn't tangle. Have patience and practice a lot. French knots can be time-consuming to make, but the overall texture you can achieve is worth it.

HOW TO

Bring the needle up through the fabric from the back side at 1. With your free hand, hold the thread with your index finger and thumb to the side. Wrap the thread around the needle front to back two times and pull gently to tighten the wraps. Keeping the thread taut, insert the point of the needle into the fabric about 2mm to the side of 1. (Down at 2.) As you push the needle through the fabric, slide the wraps down the needle against the fabric, keeping taut the thread held with your free hand. Push the needle into the fabric to from a knot.

Milliners needles are great for working French knots, as they have the same shaft thickness throughout the length of the needle, making it easier to slide the knot off.

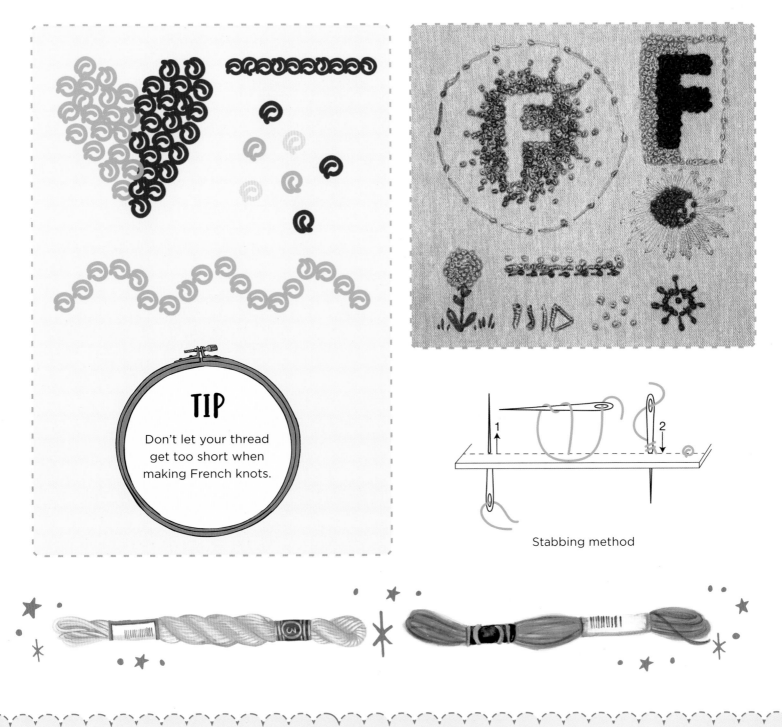

TIP

Don't let your thread get too short when making French knots.

Stabbing method

Fly Stitch

The fly stitch works well for making a border or a line with texture and movement. Try combining fly stitches of different sizes, overlapping them using different colors of thread for an interesting effect.

HOW TO

Bring the needle up through the fabric from the back side at 1. Insert the needle at 2, horizontally across from point 1, forming a small loop. Bring the needle up at 3, inside the loop. Go back down at 4 on the outside of the loop. This stitch will hold the loop in place.

Stabbing method

Sewing method

Open Fish Bone

This can be a tricky one to master, and I always have to practice it before I use it in a project. It is perfect for filling small shapes, like leaves and trees.

HOW TO

Define the shape to be filled. I like to draw two lines down the center, a few millimeters apart. Working from top to bottom, bring the needle up through the fabric from the back side at 1. Make a diagonal stitch, down at 2. Bring the needle back up at 3 and make another diagonal stitch, down at 4. Bring the thread back up at 5 and diagonal down at 6, repeating the process until the shape is filled.

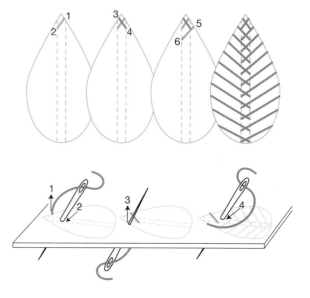

Running Stitch

Similar to the backstitch, the running stitch is for making straight or curvy lines and can be used to create fun geometric patterns. I like to use it for adding decorative details to a piece and experimenting with combining colors and shapes.

HOW TO

Working right to left, bring the needle up from the back of the fabric at 1, down at 2, back up at 3, down at 4. The stitches form a continuous line with equal-sized stitches and spaces. You can play with the stitch and space length for variety.

Although you may achieve more precise results with the stabbing method, this stitch is great for using the sewing method because it's so easy to quickly make multiple stitches.

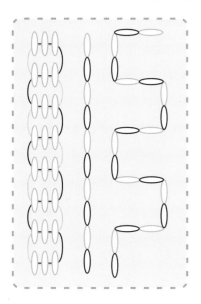  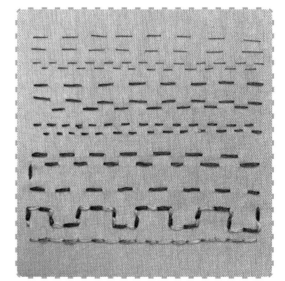

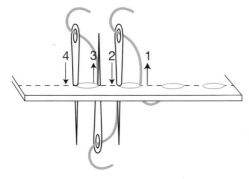

Stabbing method

Sewing method

Threaded Running Stitch

This is the same as threaded backstitch, but you start with a running stitch line.

Whipped Running Stitch

This is the same as whipped running backstitch, but you start with a running stitch line.

Satin Stitch

The trick to keeping satin stitch looking neat is to outline it with a line stitch, such as backstitch. By doing this, you can hide any imperfections and inconsistencies. Satin stitch is great for filling areas and adding a bit of dimension to shapes.

HOW TO

Define the shape to be filled. Bring the needle up through the fabric from the back side at 1. Make a stitch across the shape and insert the needle into the fabric at 2. Cross back under the shape and bring the needle up at 3, next to 1. Keep crossing over and under until the shape is filled. The stitches should be laying side by side with consistent tension so that they don't pucker.

To add dimension to the shape, stitch the outline of it first with backstitch or split stitch. Then stitch around the outline stitch using the method above to fill the shape.

To tidy up the outline of a satin stitch, stitch around the shape close to the edge with backstitch, chain stitch, or stem stitch.

Stabbing method

Sewing method

Stem Stitch

This is one of my favorite outline stitches to use. It's simple, it has a bit of texture, and it follows curves beautifully. To maneuver around tight curves, simply shorten the stitches. This stitch is perfect for script lettering, facial features, and flower stems.

HOW TO

Working from left to right, follow the design line. Bring the needle up through the fabric from the back side at 1. Make a slightly diagonal stitch, inserting the needle at 2, just outside of the design line. Bring the needle back up at 3, halfway between points 1 and 2, on the center design line. Continue making uniform stitches following the line.

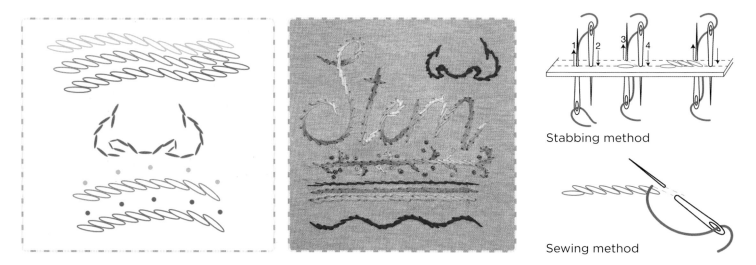

Stabbing method

Sewing method

Star Stitch

Star stitch is fun to use when creating a decorative border, filling a large shape, or making gemstones sparkle. Try using a variegated or sparkly thread to achieve a more textural effect.

HOW TO

Bring the needle up through the fabric from the back side at 1. Using straight stitches, make a cross stitch going down at 2, up at 3, down at 4. Then work a diagonal cross, up at 5, down at 6, up at 7, down at 8. Make a small cross stitch in the center to hold the star stitches in place. Up at 9, down at 10.

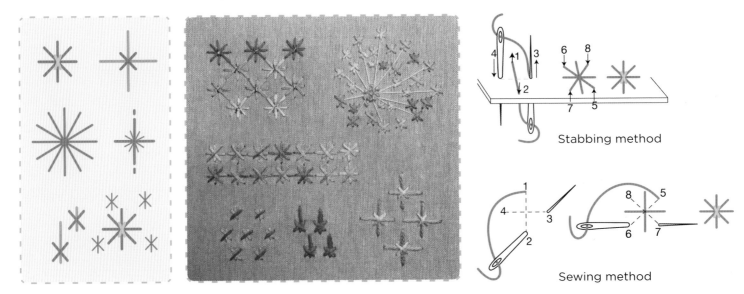

Straight Stitch

This is arguably the most versatile stitch on the planet! Straight stitches simply consist of up-and-down stitches. Vary the length as needed. When I need to fill a random space, I straight stitch! Straight stitches are ideal for building up texture and experimenting. Seed stitches are small straight stitches used to fill an area.

HOW TO

Bring the needle up through the fabric from the back side at 1 and insert the needle down at 2. Repeat, working in any direction and changing the length of the stitches as needed.

STITCH MAP

Before you begin stitching a portrait, look at the overall movement and direction in the face. Here I've used the Ruth Bader Ginsburg project that appears on pages 96-111.

With the red arrows in figure 1, you can see how I've approached stitching the face and neck, following the topography of the face. This information isn't in the transferred pattern (see pages 32-35 to learn how to transfer a design to fabric), but if you look at my final embroidery on page 111, you can use that as a reference. This is an intuitive process, so use this as a guide for stitching a face, and step back from your work often to take a break and gain perspective. When I get too close to my work, it's often difficult to see the real progress and areas where I need to pivot and change direction.

The stitch map in figure 2 shows in greater detail my approach to filling the face with color and texture. Again, use this as a guide for stitching the overall effect of a face. Use longer stitches for bigger areas of color and shorten the stitches for detailed areas, such as the eyes, nose, mouth, and ears. Your stitches will look slightly different from mine, and that's OK!

FIGURE 1

FIGURE 2

TRANSFERRING DESIGNS TO FABRIC

Whether you prefer to use the design I have provided in each project or want to get creative by adding other elements or drawing your own design, you will need to get that design transferred onto fabric. There are quite a few methods of transfer, and I've used different ones in different projects. The method you choose will depend on several factors, including the size and detail of the project, the content and color of the fabric you are using, and the tools and materials that are available to you. Take your time preparing your fabric and choosing the best method of transfer, as this will set you up for a successful (and fun!) embroidering project.

Preparing the Fabric & Hoop

Before transferring the design, I like to wash my fabric by hand or using the gentle cycle of the washing machine, and then let it dry. This will wash away any sizing or chemicals left on the fabric by the manufacturer and pre-shrink the fabric, preventing puckering or distortion of the stitches later. This is important especially if you will be washing away stabilizer or using a water-soluble pen or pencil. After pre-washing, iron your base fabric to remove any wrinkles.

At this stage, I also choose the hoop I'm going to use for my project, often opting for a larger one that will fit the entire project within the hoop so that I can see and work on it all at once, rather than shifting a smaller hoop around on the piece as I stitch.

Before committing to any of the transfer methods listed here, it's important to test them on a scrap piece of the fabric you are using. Different types of fabrics will work differently with each transfer method. Testing the transfer method will save you time, money, and heartache in the long run.

METHOD 1: WATER-SOLUBLE STABILIZER

Since I discovered the existence of water-soluble stabilizer at a workshop years ago, this has been my go-to method for transferring designs to fabric, especially if I'm working on something complex and detailed. With this material, you can copy, trace, or print the pattern directly onto the stabilizer, and then place that on your fabric. I like the sticky-back version that sticks onto the fabric, rather than pinning it down.

You can copy the black-and-white design in each project in this book onto the stabilizer sheets or use a light source to trace the image if you don't have access to a printer and copier. You can also scan the image into your computer, resize it as needed, and print onto water-soluble stabilizer.

I like Pellon® and Sulky Solvy® brands. When you are working on dark fabrics or if you have a detailed pattern, the water-soluble stabilizer method is a great option.

STEP 1
Trace, copy, or print the design of your choice onto a water-soluble stabilizer sheet. Depending on the size of the embroidery pattern, you may need to use two sheets of stabilizer. I prefer to print or copy versus tracing with pencil.

STEP 2
Peel off the backing if necessary and place the sheet firmly onto your fabric. Now you are ready to stitch your design! Remember that the stabilizer is water soluble and any drops of water will dissolve it. Very high humidity will also affect the stabilizer, so store it in a cool, dry place.

STEP 3
After stitching the design, remove the fabric from the hoop and trim off any excess stabilizer, taking care not to cut your stitches.

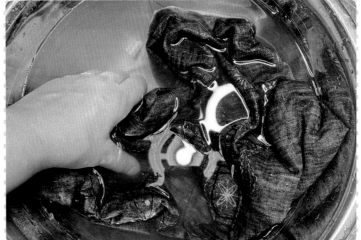

STEP 4
Soak the embroidery in warm water, gently agitating the water, and the stabilizer will dissolve away. I often use a soft, clean toothbrush to gently wash away any remaining stabilizer. After completely removing the stabilizer, lay and pin your project flat to dry.

METHOD 2: DIRECT TRACING

These methods of directly tracing the pattern onto the fabric are, for the most part, removable by heat, water, or eraser. In addition to the pens mentioned below, you could also use a sharp graphite pencil. Just be sure to test the method you choose before transferring to your fabric.

- FriXion® pen: My favorite method uses a FriXion pen by Pilot. They come in a variety of colors, and the best part is that you can use an iron to "erase" the ink if you make a mistake.

- Water-soluble pen: I prefer to use a water-soluble pen versus a marker to get more precise marks on my fabric. When using a water-soluble pen or pencil, just remember that if your fabric gets wet, the lines will disappear.

STEP 1
Print or copy the design at the size you want to embroider and tape it to your light source.

STEP 2
Place your fabric in a hoop that's large enough to fit all of the design. If the hoop is too small, you will have to reposition it to finish tracing the entire design. Using a hoop keeps the fabric taut enough to trace the lines accurately. Here I've used a FriXion pen.

STEP 3
If you make a mistake, simply iron over the ink lines. Once you finish stitching, gently iron any ink lines that still show.

METHOD 3: HOT IRON TRANSFER

There are quite a few iron-on pen and pencils available, but my absolute favorite is the Fine-Tip Iron-On Transfer Pen from Sublime Stitching®. They come in black and a variety of colors, and you can use the transfer multiple times. Just make sure to trace the reverse image of the design, especially if it has type. Otherwise, your design will transfer backwards. And remember that these pens are permanent and do not wash out. Always read the manufacturer's instructions before using transfer pens or pencils.

OTHER MATERIALS

There are many variations and methods for transferring patterns to fabric, including carbon transfer paper, stencils, and pouncing. I've outlined the three that I think best suit the projects in this book because of their complexity. Experiment and see which methods you like best! Check "Resources" on page 126-127 for my favorite materials and where to find them.

STEP 1
Print or copy the image you want to transfer and tape it to your light source. You will need to reverse the image when using transfer pens or pencils.

STEP 2
Trace the reverse image onto copy or tracing paper. I prefer using copy paper, but you can experiment to find what works for you.

STEP 3
Iron the image onto preheated fabric with a hot iron. Gently lift a corner of the paper to see if it transferred. If not, keep ironing, taking care not to shift the paper around.

FRIDA KAHLO

FRIDA KAHLO was a self-taught Mexican painter who grew to be one of the most influential artists of her generation. Known for her self-portraits, Frida produced dramatic depictions of her physical and emotional pain, but through her art, she turned pain into beauty. After a horrific bus accident and multiple surgeries, she spent months recovering in bed, where her mother rigged a special easel and mirror so that Frida could paint lying down. Despite her lifelong suffering, she was resilient and never stopped doing what she loved.

You can use the image on page 39 to embroider your portrait of Frida Kahlo, or spend some time researching Frida and make your portrait of her your own! One way to gather inspiration is to do an online image search. Lots of images of Frida Kahlo will pop up; use those as references when drawing her!

Notice the flowers in Frida Kahlo's paintings, as well as the patterns and details in her clothing and in the backgrounds of her paintings. Perhaps you can change out the accessories in one painting to those seen in another one.

By observing the details in Frida Kahlo's paintings, you can get to know her better and may feel inspired to add the elements that are meaningful to you into your own embroidery.

Other items you may want to sketch and embroider include flower varieties, such as calla lilies, poppies, marigolds, sunflowers, magnolias, and fuchsias; butterflies; parrots; monkeys; floral headbands; and items from her studio.

Stitch & Color Guide

The embroideries and patterns in this book are designed to be playful and flexible to suit your taste and stitching style. Here are a few ways to interpret the pattern with stitches. These are just suggestions to get started, though! Use this as a starting point; then let your imagination go wild. Don't want a yellow flower? Change it! Want to use a different pink color? Go for it!

Threads & Stitches

Gather the threads you'll need and plan out how you want to approach this design. This is a detailed embroidery, and I find that a good way to approach this project is to think about it in layers. What elements overlap each other? Work on the bottom layers first and build up color and textures. It's OK to be playful and expressive! Each DMC color is listed below, but you might want to see what colors you have in your collection and use those first, substituting as you want. Use different threads and yarns for added texture.

THREAD COLOR GUIDE

1 DMC 906	4 DMC 3820	7 DMC 955	10 DMC 601	13 DMC 606	16 DMC 869	19 DMC 310
2 DMC 907	5 DMC Blanc	8 DMC 311	11 DMC 894	14 DMC 783	17 DMC 758	
3 DMC 727	6 DMC 959	9 DMC 321	12 DMC 352	15 DMC 444	18 DMC 413	

STITCHES USED

BS=backstitch
SS=straight stitch
DCS=detached chain stitch
STM=stem stitch
FK=French knot
SAT=satin stitch

Pattern

Use your method of choice to transfer this design to your fabric. Keep as many details as you want, leaving some out or adding your own!

Flowers & Leaves

When embroidering motifs like flowers, consider their layers. Embroider the flower on the bottom layer first, then the yellow overlapping one. Stitch the flower petals first, then the leaves, to create a nice, layered look. Add the center of the flower last. You can embroider just the outlines of the designs or fill in the petals with color to create a more dramatic design.

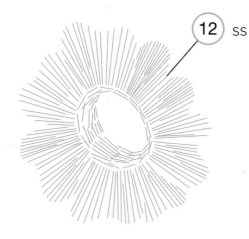 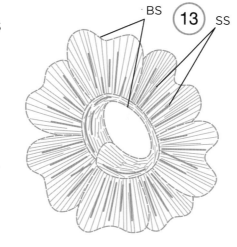 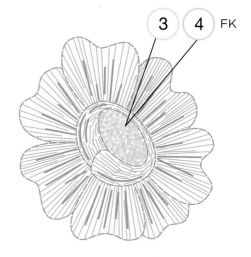

12 SS

BS 13 SS

3 4 FK

STEP 1
Fill in the petals with satin and/or straight stitch.

STEP 2
Outline using backstitch; then add details using straight stitch.

STEP 3
Fill in the center using two shades of yellow and French knots.

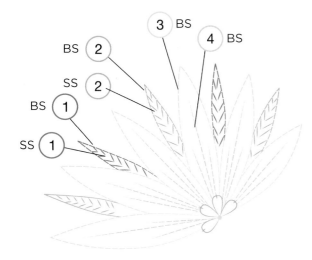

STEP 4
Fill in the petals with straight stitches.

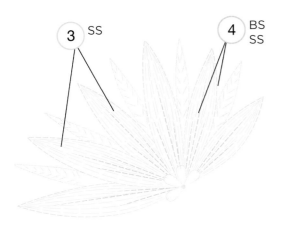

STEP 5
Outline with backstitch.

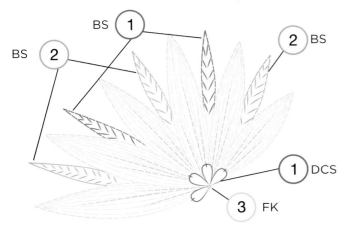

STEP 6
Fill in the leaves with straight stitches and outline with backstitch.

(11) SAT

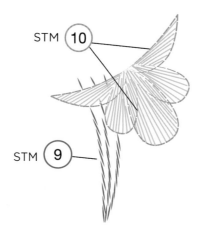

STM (10)

STM (9)

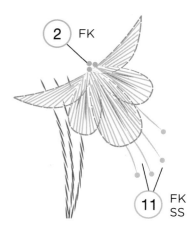

(2) FK

(11) FK
SS

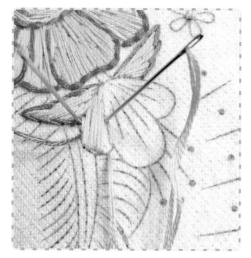

STEP 7
Fill in the petal with satin stitch.

STEP 8
Outline with stem stitch.

STEP 9
Add details with straight stitch and French knots, as well as a few French knots to form the center of the flower.

Finishing the Flower Crown

If you'd like, you can stitch the smaller flowers as you stitch the larger flowers around the flower crown. This way, you won't have to change out your needle and thread as much! The little flowers are really fun to make, so feel free to add more!

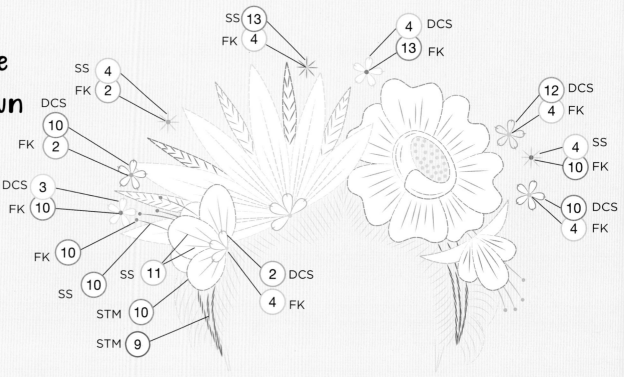

Hair & Accessories

When embroidering faces, it's usually best to keep things simple. I like using backstitch for facial features, varying the lengths of my stitches as needed for details. Below are different options for Frida's eyes, nose, and mouth. Try practicing these facial features on a scrap piece of fabric first.

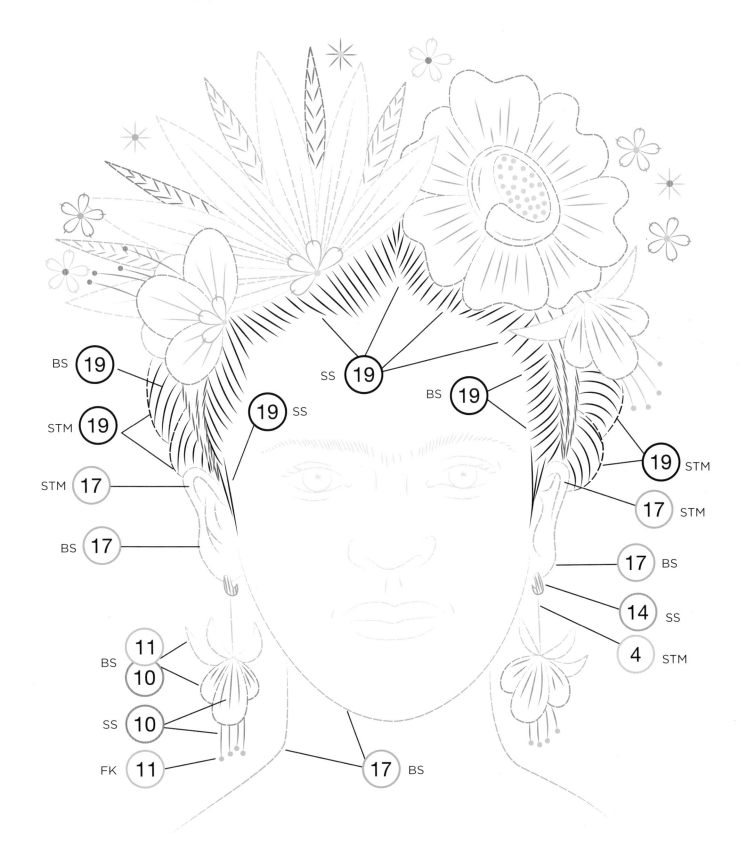

STEP 1
Use a combination of backstitch and straight stitch, varying the lengths of the stitches.

STEP 2
Outline the ear with backstitch. You can add a bit more pink as well for more depth if you like.

STEP 3
Outline the chin and neck with backstitch, again adding pink for depth.

Eyes & Eyebrows

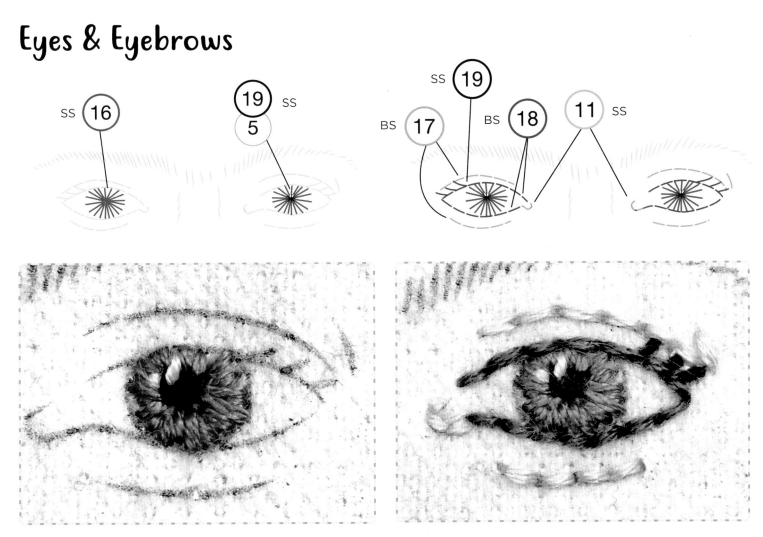

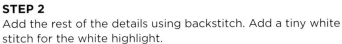

STEP 1
Fill in the iris with straight stitch. Start in the center and radiate outward. Outline the iris with brown backstitch and add a star stitch in the center for the pupil.

STEP 2
Add the rest of the details using backstitch. Add a tiny white stitch for the white highlight.

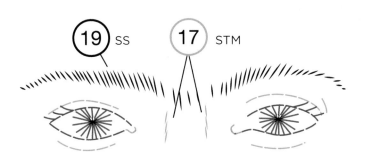

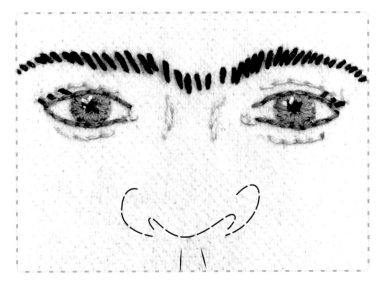

STEP 3
Add the bridge of the nose with a few small slip stitches. Then create the eyebrows with small straight stitches.

Nose & Mouth

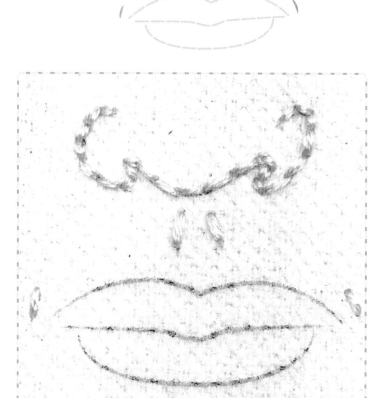

BS **17**

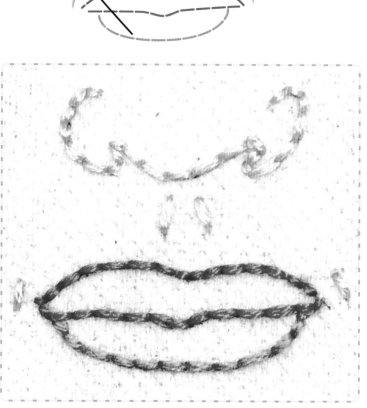

BS **10**

STEP 1

Use one color for the nose, plus a bit of pink on the tip if you'd like. Use backstitches of varying lengths to accommodate the curves.

STEP 2

Outline the lips using small red backstitches. To add more dimension, fill in the lips using straight stitches.

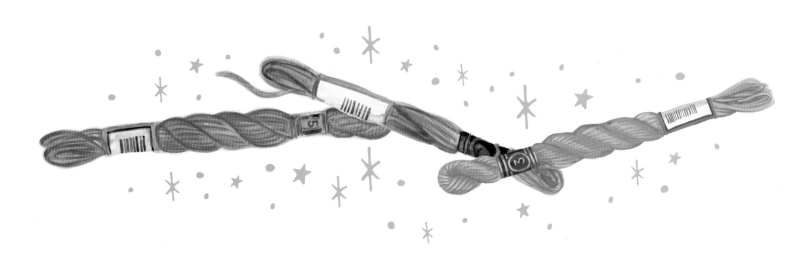

Necklaces & Banner

This area is very layered, so approach it by working from the bottom layer up. Embroider the pink and red trim on the shirt first, as well as the golden necklaces. Then add the dark green trim and outline. Finish with the blue necklace and the hummingbird and banner.

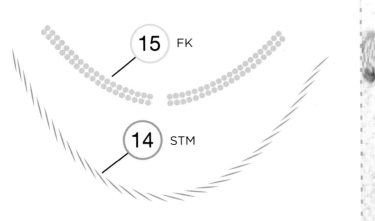

STEP 1
Stitch two rows of French knots very close together to form the first necklace. The darker gold necklace consists of one row of stem stitches. You could also experiment with metallic thread here.

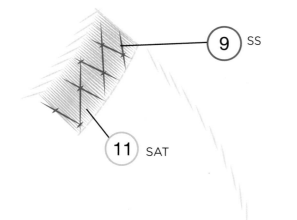

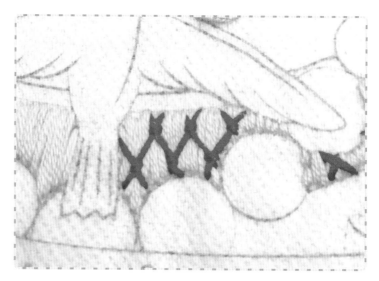

STEP 2

Start with light pink using satin stitch to fill the neckline. Add long straight stitches on top of the satin stitches to form the diamond pattern; then add a small straight stitch at the intersections to hold down the long stitches.

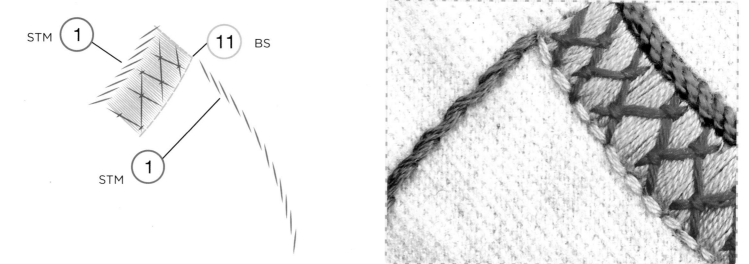

STEP 3

Add back stitches around the edge of the pink collar; then add a stem stitch in green to form the outline of the shirt.

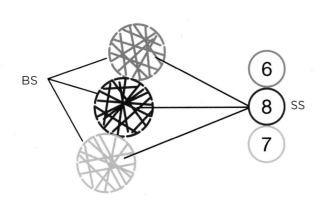

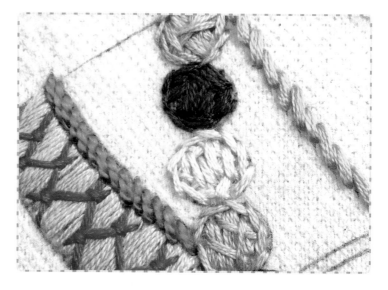

STEP 4

Outline each bead of the necklace in backstitch. Fill each bead with "sloppy" straight stitches to add fun texture and dimension.

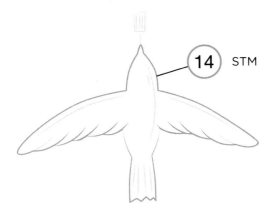

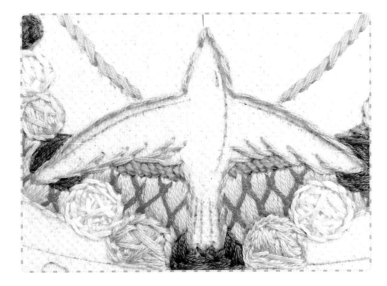

STEP 5

Outline the hummingbird using small stem stitches.

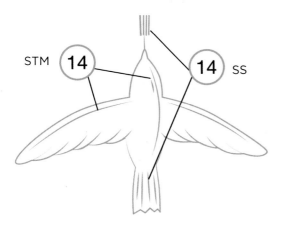

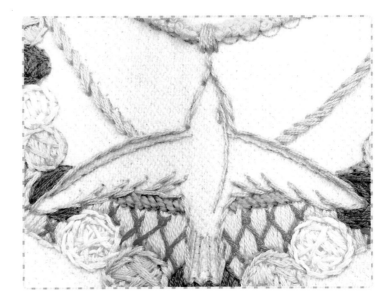

STEP 6

Add details with stem stitches. Use one or two strands of thread to create dimension, and add final details with straight stitches.

STEP 7

Using small stem stitches, outline the letters, or use backstitch. Add a French knot to dot the "i."

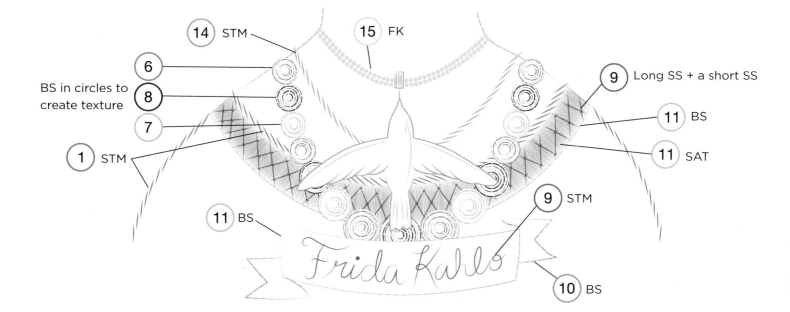

14 STM
15 FK
6
BS in circles to create texture
8
7
1 STM
9 Long SS + a short SS
11 BS
11 SAT
11 BS
9 STM
10 BS

Frida Kahlo

STEP 8
Outline the banner using backstitch.

Frida Kahlo

ELEANOR ROOSEVELT

ELEANOR ROOSEVELT was born in 1884 in New York City. She became the longest-serving First Lady of the United States and fought fiercely for the poor, workers, women and youth groups, Japanese-Americans, miners, and the Civil Rights movement. She expanded the traditional role of First Lady into one that gave her time to write, teach, and pursue reform politics. Eleanor used her privilege to enact change and advocate for those who suffered the most.

"DO ONE THING EVERY DAY THAT SCARES YOU."

Eleanor Roosevelt lived a full and expansive life, and you will find a lot of information about her online. Read biographies of her life as an activist, a writer, and a humanitarian. Study quotes from her that you find inspiring.

Suggestions include:

"You must do the thing you think you cannot do."

"Do one thing every day that scares you."

"The giving of love is an education in itself."

"The future belongs to those who believe in the beauty of their dreams."

"It is not fair to ask of others what you are not willing to do yourself."

Doing an online image search for Eleanor Roosevelt will bring up lots of pictures of her in clothing, hats, and jewelry that tell the story of her time.

Other things you might want to sketch and embroider in a portrait of Eleanor Roosevelt include the White House or a portrait of Eleanor with her husband, President Franklin D. Roosevelt.

Eleanor Roosevelt

Eleanor Roosevelt

ELEANOR

Stitch & Color Guide

I've taken inspiration for the colors in this project from photos of the time period in which Eleanor Roosevelt lived: black and white; soft, warm grays; and muted colors. The stitches are simple, and I've used a loosely woven natural cotton with some slubby pieces in it. I've used DMC cottons, but the softness of the piece could also be reinforced with beautiful wool threads.

Threads & Stitches

Gather the threads you'll need and plan how you want to approach this design. You can follow the threads I've used or choose a different color scheme to suit your style. I love looking at old photos of Eleanor Roosevelt to get inspired, and then interpreting those images into colored stitches.

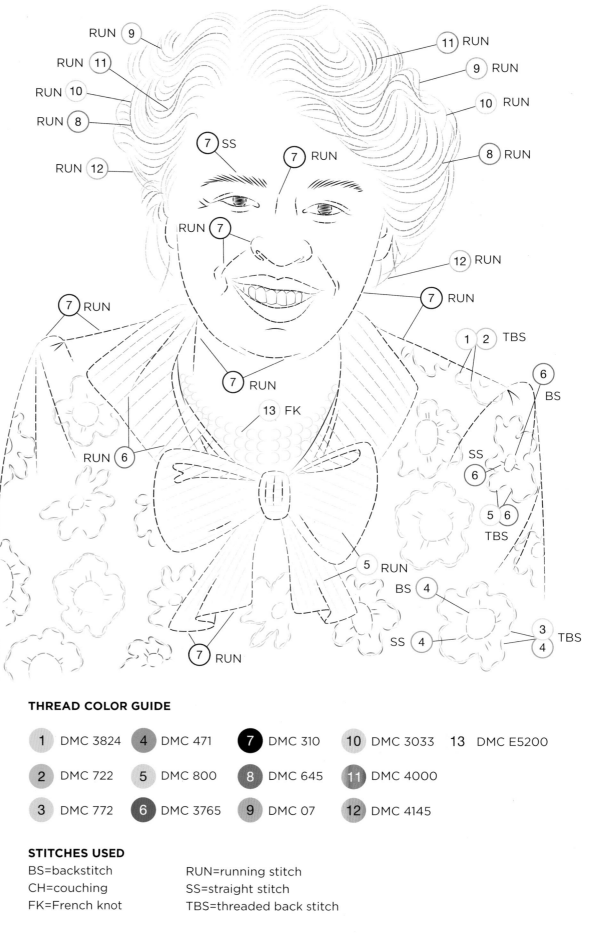

THREAD COLOR GUIDE

1 DMC 3824	**4** DMC 471	**7** DMC 310	**10** DMC 3033	**13** DMC E5200
2 DMC 722	**5** DMC 800	**8** DMC 645	**11** DMC 4000	
3 DMC 772	**6** DMC 3765	**9** DMC 07	**12** DMC 4145	

STITCHES USED

BS=backstitch
CH=couching
FK=French knot

RUN=running stitch
SS=straight stitch
TBS=threaded back stitch

Pattern

When transferring this design, consider using different textures on the blouse, collar, and bow, or adding to the background. I've kept the details fairly simple, but you should feel free to add more details if you'd like. Include any of Eleanor's powerful quotes, her name in a 1940s font, or a fun picture frame using a simple stitch.

Face

To embroider the face for this project, I've used mostly running stitches of varying sizes and one color (black) for the facial features. Experiment with adding soft pinks to the lips or other skin tones.

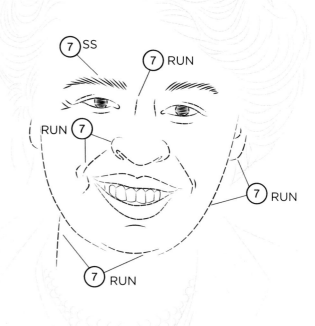

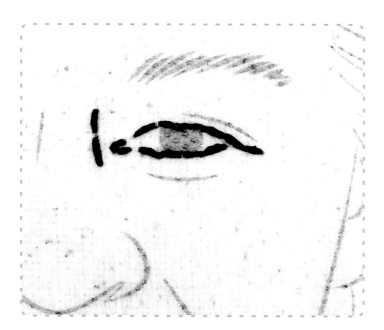

STEP 1

Outline the eyes with small backstitches and use a few straight stitches for the corner. Keep it simple here!

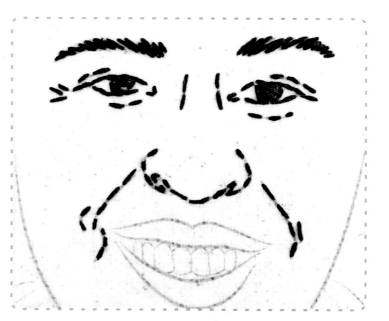

STEP 2

Outline the iris with a few small backstitches and fill with straight stitches or satin stitch. Add the creases of the eyes using running stitch and fill in the brows with straight stitches.

STEP 3

Outline the nose and creases of the cheeks with running stitch. To navigate the tight curves of the nostrils, shorten your stitches. Again, keep it simple!

Mouth Options

As with all of my patterns, you have the freedom to change up the colors, stitches, elements, and layout. Here are a few options for the mouth that I stitched on scrap fabric before finally landing on the simplicity of a black line. I've used straight stitches to fill the lips with color.

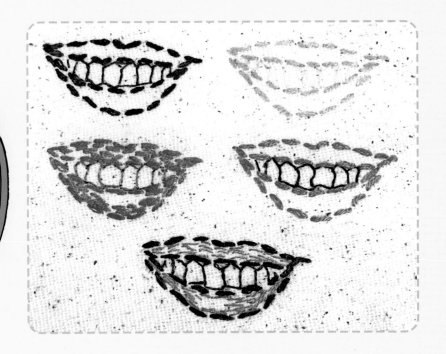

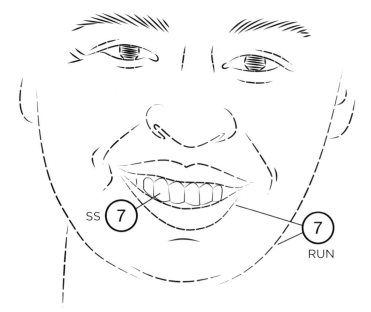

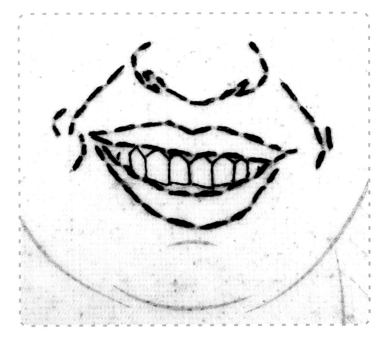

STEP 4

Outline the lips using running stitch. I've used one strand of thread to outline the teeth with straight stitches. I suggest looking at some photos of Eleanor smiling to get a good sense of the structure of her mouth and teeth.

Hair

Eleanor Roosevelt's hair is a mix of soft, warm grays and browns. It's not essential to stitch each strand exactly as I have; rather, you want to capture the shadows and light to create the forms of the hair. I've used three strands of DMC cotton. You can also use one or two strands to indicate some of the wispy strands around her face. All of the stitches are running stitch, but you can substitute any other type of outline stitch, such as backstitch or stem stitch.

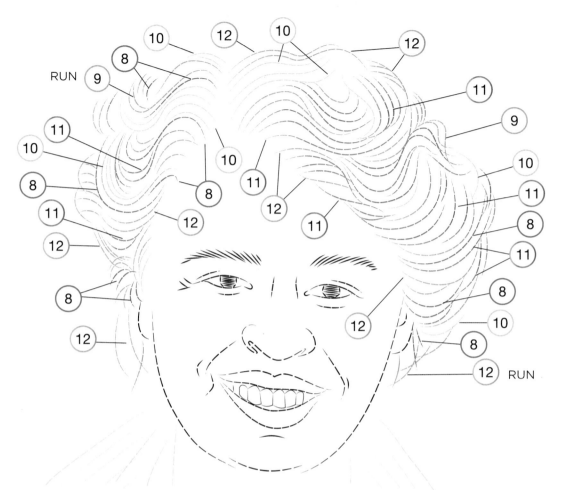

STEP 1

Stitch light-colored strands of hair using the lightest tone and light variegated thread. Add a medium tone to build volume.

STEP 2

Layer in the darker tones to build shadows. Using a dark variegated thread is a great way to add several colors to the stitches.

STEP 3

Continue to build volume with medium and dark thread colors.

STEP 4

Finish adding any light-colored stitches that need to be filled. You can also fill in with darker colors to finish off the hair if necessary. For some of the wispy hairs around the face, use two strands instead of three to create variety in the texture.

Shirt, Collar & Bow

Keep the stitching consistent when outlining the blouse. A simple running stitch will unify the entire design, but you should feel free to use different types of threads or yarns to make it even more special. I've used a metallic and cotton blend for the bow to add a bit of sparkle.

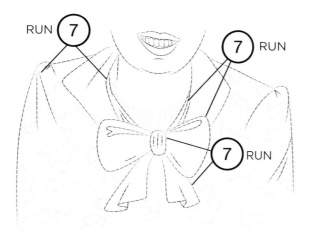

STEP 1

Stitch the outlines of the shirt, collar, and bow using running stitch.

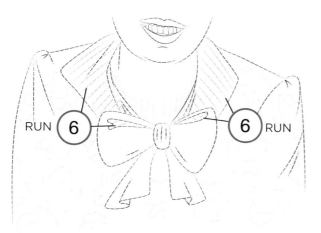

STEP 2

Add the darker blue in the collar. You can use the same color inside the bow to create a shadow effect.

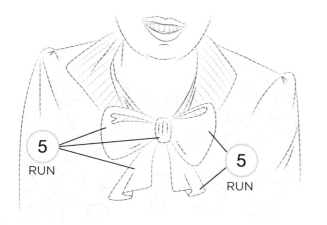

STEP 3

I've added a bit of sparkle in the bow using a special multistrand thread. One of the strands is metallic.

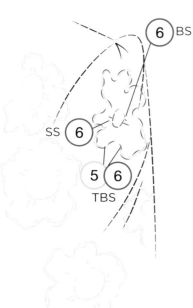

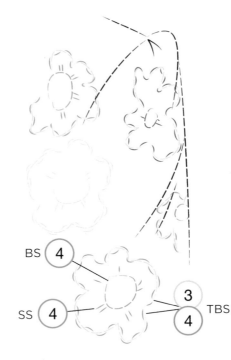

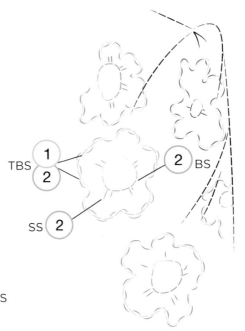

STEP 4
Outline the flower with light-blue backstitch. Thread the darker blue through the backstitch without piercing the fabric, carefully maneuvering in the corners. This is the threaded backstitch. Add the straight stitch details to the center.

STEP 5
Using the same method as in step 4, stitch the green flower with the light green first, followed by the dark green.

STEP 6
Finish by stitching the orange flowers with light and dark colors. You can also add small seed stitches to the shirt for more detail, or just keep it simple with flowers.

Necklace

Eleanor Roosevelt often wore strands of pearls or other necklaces. You can use interesting-looking yarn or beads to interpret these necklaces. See what you have in your materials, and experiment with different looks. Below are three different ways to interpret the pearl necklaces. Have fun with them and use some practice fabric to play before stitching your piece!

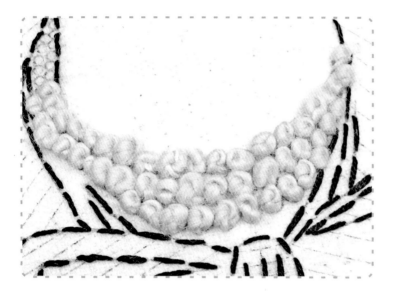

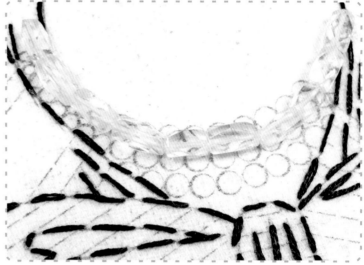

OPTION 1

Here I've used beautiful hand-spun wool yarn. If you go a similar route, make sure to use the right size needle. I've used a needle for ribbon embroidery that has a large eye to accommodate the thick yarn, as well as French knots. For the larger knots, I've wrapped the wool twice around the needle, and with the smaller ones, I've wrapped once.

OPTION 2

You can also stitch beads or faux pearls onto the fabric. Here I've used just one strand of beads, but you could try different sizes of beads and create more strands. I've used a size 10 beading needle and one strand of DMC white thread.

OPTION 3

Here I've used French knots again, but with a six-strand thread that is iridescent (DMC E5200). This thread is more difficult to work with and often gets tangled, especially on the back, but I love the look of it! I've used three strands here.

Typography

Sketch out Eleanor's name and your favorite quotes from her before adding them to your portrait. Stitches that work well for embroidering type include backstitch, chain stitch, and couching.

Finishing Your Embroidery

After you've finished stitching the necklaces, step back from your work and decide if you want to add anything else...perhaps a hand-stitched quote or more textures? Sometimes less is more, so you might be finished! I've used printed water-soluble stabilizer, so I rinse and soak it in water, and then dry flat.

The Back Side of the Embroidery

I'm showing you the back side of this embroidery for a couple of reasons. I've used quite a bit of black thread, so you'll notice that I didn't carry the thread over long distances. This prevents the thread from getting stuck or snagged on things. Because the fabric weave is more open and lighter in color, you won't see the threads showing through the front. I've used a combination of small knots and the weaving method to finish my stitches. Either way is perfectly fine in my book! I do like to keep the back fairly tidy, but I'm not obsessive about it. You'll notice a few spots where my thread got a bit tangled, but I've done my best to tuck it back in and keep stitching.

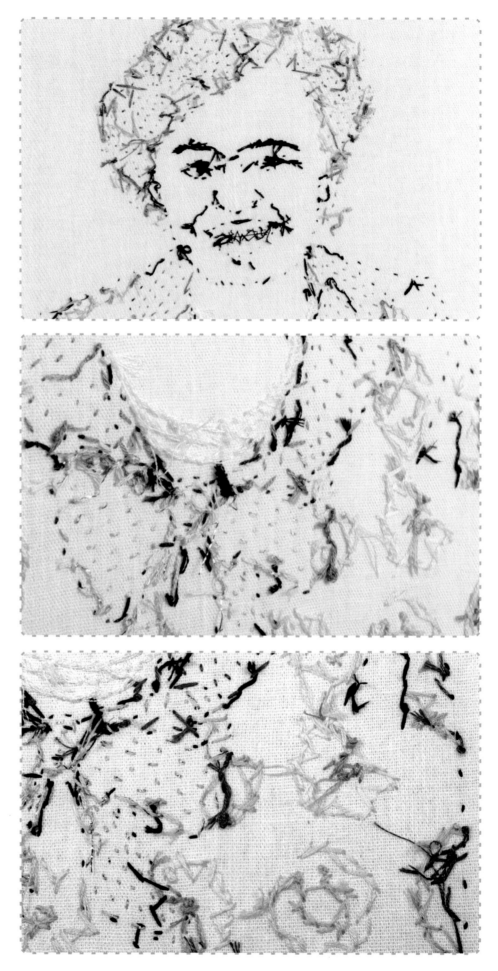

MAYA ANGELOU

MAYA ANGELOU was many things in her lifetime, including a poet, an actress, a screenwriter, a dancer, and a civil rights activist. Maya experienced prejudice and racism while growing up in the South, and these experiences led her to help her friends Malcolm X and Martin Luther King Jr. fight racial injustice. Maya Angelou used the power of her words to champion equality for Black women and men. In her books, including the internationally acclaimed *I Know Why the Caged Bird Sings*, Maya Angelou explores issues of identity, family, rape, racism, the struggle for freedom, and literacy. In spite of a life filled with sadness, death, and racial abuse, Maya traveled the world and became a strong survivor, inspiring many lives with her writing and speaking.

Born in the month of April, Maya Angelou's birth-month flowers are the daisy and the sweet pea. Flowers are great for borders, details to fill space, and as I have done, definition in the letters of a name.

Maya Angelou was incredibly active throughout her life, and there is an abundance of imagery to reference when drawing ideas. Doing a quick online image search will yield many references, but you can also watch documentaries and read interviews and Maya's books for inspiration as well.

I've read that her favorite color was pink and that her favorite words were "joy" and "love." It's easy to incorporate some of Maya Angelou's words, phrases, and quotes into your embroidery designs and use them to fill shapes or spaces.

Maya's writing rituals included a bottle of sherry, a yellow legal pad, a thesaurus, a Bible, and the game of solitaire when she needed a break. These are all great items to incorporate into embroidered stories about her.

She recited a poem at President Bill Clinton's inauguration, and President Barack Obama awarded her the Presidential Medal of Freedom in 2010.

Phrases to embroider:
"You can't use up creativity. The more you use, the more you have."

"You may kill me with your hatefulness. But still, like air, I'll rise."

Phenomenal woman. That's me.

"I KNOW WHY THE CAGED BIRD SINGS."

Stitch & Color Guide

I've chosen a gorgeous mustard-colored linen to stitch this portrait of Maya Angelou. It's a nice midrange neutral to stitch on and works well with so many colors. By performing an online image search for "Maya Angelou fashion" or "Maya Angelou dress," you will find lots of inspiration for color, pattern, and texture to use in your designs if you want to customize this piece.

Influenced by African and European cultures, Angelou was always impeccably dressed, from her pearls and head wraps to patterned dresses.

Threads & Stitches

This project, like so many others in this book, is a great opportunity to experiment with pattern, texture, and color. Play with using contrasting colors, like orange and blue or a range of greens, for the head wrap and blouse Maya Angelou wears. Experiment and practice on a piece of scrap fabric with different colors to work out your color scheme, or feel free to follow the colors and stitches I've used.

THREAD COLOR GUIDE

1 DMC 869	**4** DMC 317	**7** DMC 22	**10** DMC 783	**13** DMC 4015	**16** DMC 518	**19** DMC 4190
2 DMC 3031	**5** DMC BLANC	**8** DMC 3859	**11** MET GOLD	**14** DMC 4065	**17** DMC 336	**20** DMC 891
3 DMC 310	**6** DMC 498	**9** DMC 4000	**12** DMC 3822	**15** DMC 4126	**18** DMC 69	**21** DMC 4070

STITCHES USED

BS=backstitch
CH=couching
CS=chain stitch

DCS=detached chain stitch
FK=French knot
RUN=running stitch
SS=straight stitch

STM=stem stitch
TBS=threaded backstitch
TRS=threaded running stitch

Pattern

When transferring this design, consider embroidering a quote from Maya Angelou in the background or below the portrait in place of her name and flowers.

Face

I've kept the details simple in Maya Angelou's face, but small details are important—the twinkle in her eye, the way her lips turn up slightly at the corners. I've used three strands for most of the face, but if you'd like to add a few more expressive details or areas of shadow, you can switch over to one strand of thread. I like to keep the face simple and add more detail to the rest of the image.

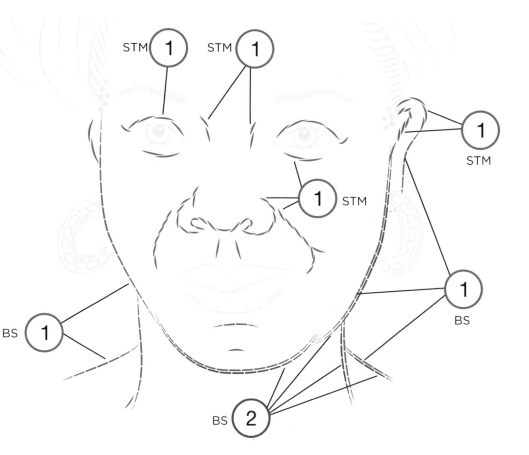

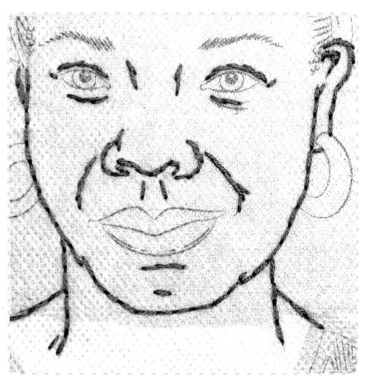

STEP 1

Using backstitch, embroider the outlines of the face, including the upper eyelid. Use stem stitches to embroider the facial details, shortening the stitches around small curves. Use small straight stitches for details like creases by the mouth and eyes.

STEP 2

To give areas of the face a little more definition, outline them using a darker thread. I've used dark brown, but a deep, dark purple or midnight blue would be great too. If you want to add more detail in this stage, switch to a single strand.

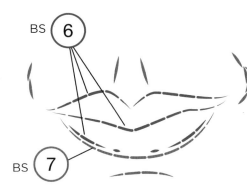

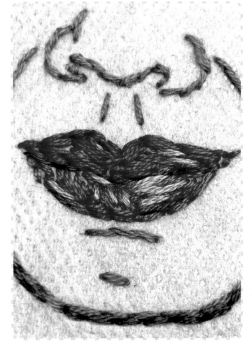

STEP 3

Outline the lips using dark maroon and medium red. Adjust the size of the backstitches as you maneuver around corners and creases.

STEP 4

Fill the upper and lower lips with two shades of red using different sizes of straight stitches. The upper lip is darker here. Overlap the stitches as needed, changing direction to show dimension.

STEP 5

Add highlight stitches using the lightest red or pink color. With two strands of the darkest brown, use straight stitches to add a bit of definition between the lips and a tiny bit of shadow around the edges.

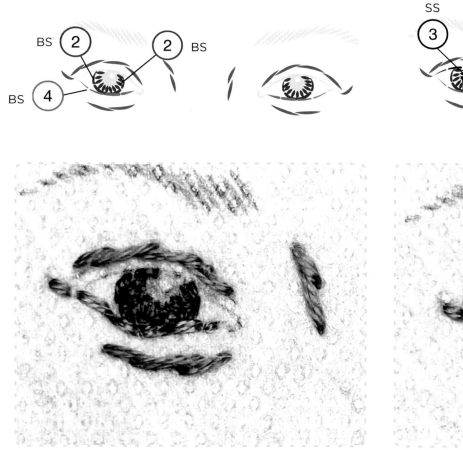

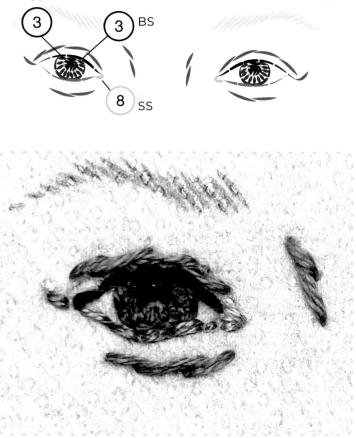

STEP 6

Using two strands, outline the iris with backstitch and fill the area with small straight stitches. Leave room for the black pupil. Outline the bottom eyelid with dark gray thread.

STEP 7

Add black straight stitches for the pupil and backstitch for the upper eyelid. Add small straight stitches for the inner corner of the eye.

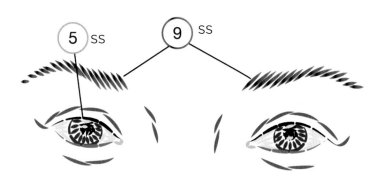

STEP 8

You may need to use a thimble here to push the needle through the layers of stitches. Using two strands of white thread, add small straight stitches to indicate the whites of the eyes. Add a few tiny stitches as highlights on the pupils. Stitch the eyebrows using straight stitches.

TIP

Another option is to research Maya Angelou's various hairstyles and add hair to the portrait instead of a head wrap.

Hair, Head Wrap & Earrings

As you may have noticed, I love using variegated threads! You can achieve so many different shades and tones using just one thread. The head wrap on Maya Angelou is a great place to play with color and texture, using different thicknesses and colors of threads and yarns. You will notice that in my final embroidery, I've added more pattern and texture to the head wrap.

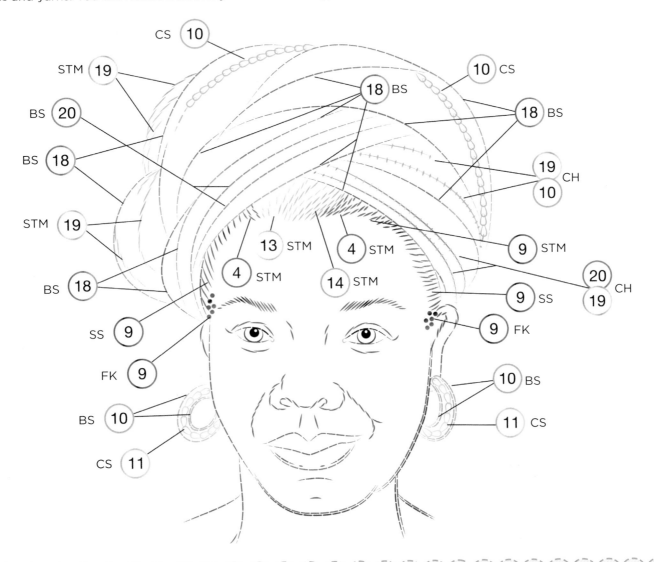

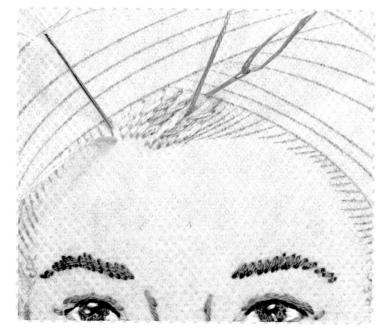

STEP 1

Stitch light-colored strands of hair using the lightest and medium variegated threads. Feel free to add more stitches to fill in spaces if necessary. For areas like the hair, where I'm "painting" with color, I usually have a couple of needles going at the same time. It's a fun way to stitch; just make sure to keep the threads from tangling.

STEP 2

Layer in the medium and dark colors using stem and straight stitches as needed. Add French knots for texture.

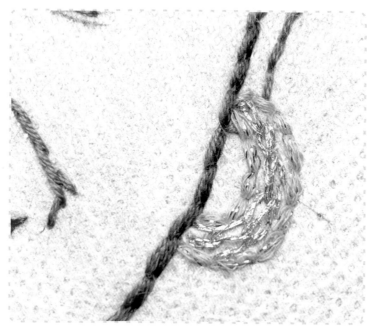

STEP 3

Outline the earrings with backstitch. Here I've used DMC Moline Etoile (C725) because it has a little sparkle. Fill the earrings with metallic gold thread using chain stitch. If you need to fill in space, add another row or two with backstitch or straight stitch.

STEP 4

Using backstitch, outline the head wrap. Here I've used a beautiful hand-dyed wool yarn (right) to give the stitches a chunky look. Add more details using chain stitch, stem stitch, and couching. Continue to embellish the head wrap with fun patterns if you'd like.

Shirt & Text Outline

If you are using printed water-soluble stabilizer, as I do on most of my work, you will notice that over time it may shift around a bit. On larger pieces like portraits, I often use pins to keep the stabilizer in place. In this portrait, I've also stitched down the "Maya" text using a single strand of floss and backstitch. This helps neatly outline the text and keeps the stabilizer from shifting too much.

Take some time to research the creative outfits that Maya Angelou wore as an actress, a singer, and a writer in places like Egypt, Ghana, and the United States. Her clothes were colorful and authentic, and you will take much inspiration from them. This is where you can also have a lot of fun with embellishments, such as seed beads or sequins, to add color and texture.

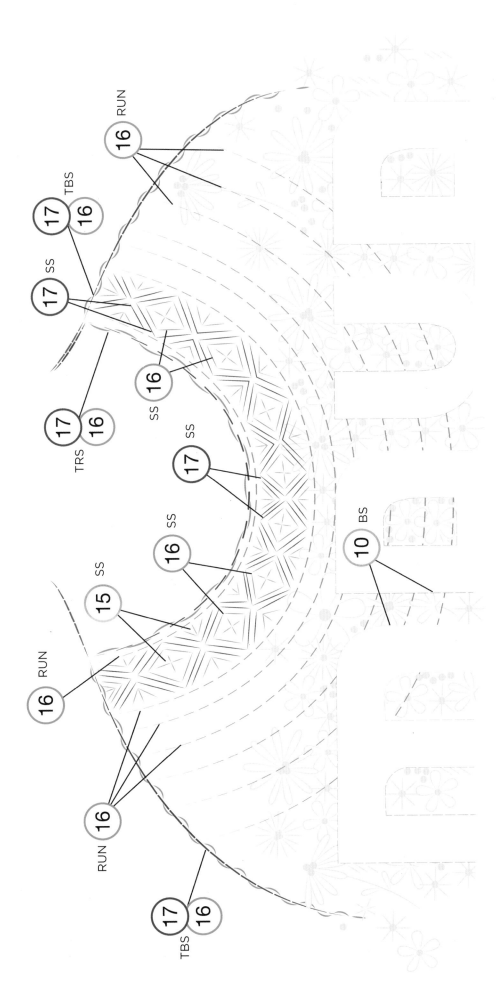

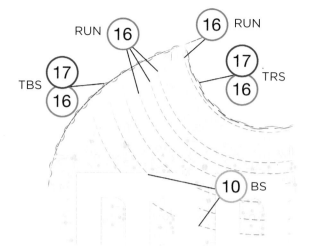

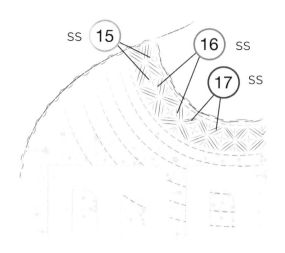

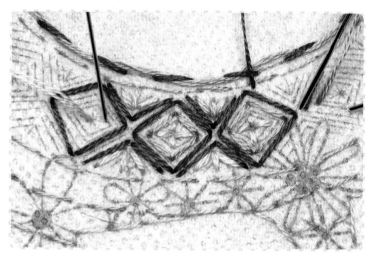

STEP 1

Start by outlining the shirt using stitches that give a bit of texture: threaded backstitch and running stitch. Alternatively, you can also use whipped stitches. The outline of "Maya" and light-blue detail stitches use a single strand of thread. Later you will embroider flowers on top of portions of the blue lines.

STEP 2

Because this is a complex area, I've used two strands of thread for each color. It's fun to have several needles going at once, but you can also embroider each color one by one using straight stitches.

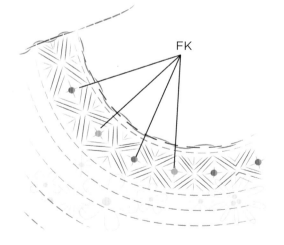

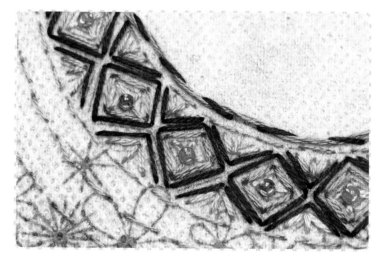

STEP 3

If you'd like, you can add extra detail by stitching on some colorful beads or adding French knots here for more sparkle and texture.

Flowers & Type

I've chosen daisies from Maya Angelou's birth month of April to give shape to the name "Maya" in this portrait. Feel free to experiment if you want to add sweet peas (the other birth flower from the month of April) to the mix as well. You can also leave off "Angelou" if you'd like and add even more flowers!

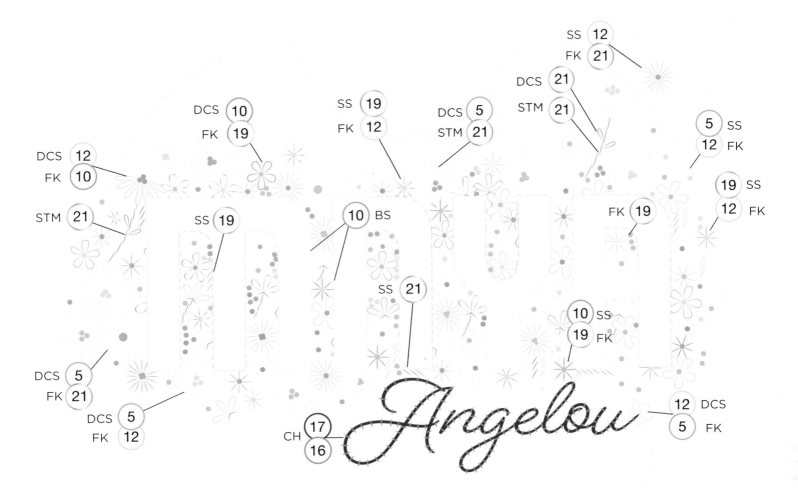

STEP 1

Embroidering the flowers is a really fun step in this project. I've used a variety of stitches for the daisies, including detached chain stitch, French knots, and straight stitches. You can add other types of flowers too for extra variety. A simple yet stunning effect to try is using only two colors—for example, white and yellow—with a variety of threads and yarns.

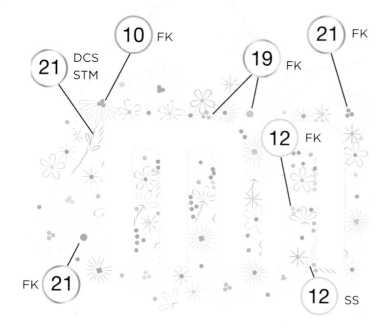

21 DCS STM
10 FK
21 FK
19 FK
12 FK
21 FK
12 FK
12 SS

17 CH
16
12 DCS
5 FK

Angelou

STEP 2

Continue to fill in the areas around the name "Maya" with flowers, stems, and filler stitches, including straight stitches and French knots. As you can see, I've added extra-bright colors and fun yarns for more texture. Be playful and have fun!

STEP 3

Use couching stitch to embroider "Angelou" in two colors. Feel free to draw the type in your own handwriting or switch up the colors. Chain stitch is another great option here.

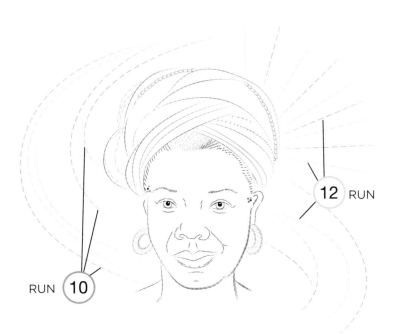

RUN (10)

(12) RUN

STEP 4

Embroider the swirls in the background, or keep the look simple and leave them off. Here I've used a simple running stitch with two strands.

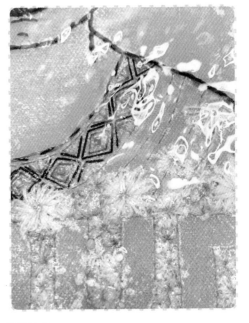

STEP 5

If you are using water-soluble stabilizer to transfer your pattern to the fabric, you can wash it off now. To reduce the amount of stabilizer you have to wash out, carefully trim off as much excess as you can. If you are using a different method of image transfer, go to step 7.

STEP 6

Wash off the water-soluble stabilizer using lukewarm to warm water. I use a soft, new toothbrush to gently wipe off all the little bits, rather than rubbing the fabric together, to avoid disturbing the stitches. Stretch and dry the fabric.

STEP 7

After the fabric has dried, gently iron the back. Decide if you want to add more details and flowers to your piece. I've added more flowers and stitches around the word "Maya" to fill in the empty spaces. This is a great time to add any beads or other embellishments if you wish!

Finishing Your Embroidery

Sometimes it's difficult to know when to stop stitching. I'm a bit of a maximalist, so I love adding more stitches and embellishments, and often I struggle to simplify. By leaving out details, however, you allow the viewer to fill them in. Do what feels right for yourself and your stitching style. More isn't always better...or is it? Step away from your work for a few hours or days and just let it be. You'll come back with a fresh perspective and you will know if you need to add anything to the piece or if it's truly complete.

The Back Side of the Embroidery

I love the back side of an embroidery almost as much as, if not more than, the front! It has a visual language all its own, almost like a shorthand version or an abstraction of the front. I try to keep the back sides of my pieces as neat as possible, but I don't let that hinder my progress. It's mainly a matter of managing threads, and over time, you'll figure out how best to do this. The main reason I like to keep the back tidy is so that threads don't come loose, pop up through the front, or get lumpy. There's a lot of debate regarding knotting your threads. I don't mind knots, although I like to keep them small and tuck the tails under my stitches.

Angelou

HARRIET TUBMAN

HARRIET TUBMAN was born around 1820 to enslaved parents. Conductor of the Underground Railroad, leading abolitionist, nurse, spy, and suffragist, Harriet escaped to freedom in 1849 and rescued and led dozens of enslaved people from Maryland to freedom in the North. One of her greatest achievements was the raid at the Combahee River, where Tubman and Union soldiers rescued more than 700 enslaved people working on nearby plantations. Harriet Tubman died on March 10, 1913, of pneumonia. She was buried with military honors at Fort Hill Cemetery in New York.

Born Araminta Ross, she married a free Black man named John Tubman, taking his last name and changing her name to Harriet. Worried that she and the other slaves on the plantation where she lived were going to be sold, Tubman ran away to freedom, settling in Philadelphia.

She rescued dozens of enslaved people from Maryland and assisted others in making their way to Canada. As her reputation in the abolitionist community grew, she became acquainted with Frederick Douglass and John Brown.

Harriet Tubman became an outspoken advocate for African-American and women's rights, insisting that all be afforded dignity, treated with respect, and granted equality.

It's believed that Harriet personally led at least 70 enslaved people to freedom, including her elderly parents, and instructed dozens of others on how to escape on their own. She once said, "I never ran my train off the track and I never lost a passenger."

Tubman depended on her great intellect, courage, and religious faith to escape slavery and rescue others. She followed rivers that snaked northward and used the stars and other natural markers to guide her. She relied on sympathetic people, Black and White, who helped her to hide, told her which way to go, and connected her with other people whom she could trust.

Tubman was an ardent suffragist and began appearing at suffrage conventions before the Civil War, becoming more active as the 19th century wore on. She fought for civil and political rights for not only women and minorities, but seniors and people with disabilities too, and she established a nursing home for African Americans.

EVERY GREAT DREAM BEGINS WITH A DREAMER.

Harriet

Stitch & Color Guide

Before beginning your piece, do a bit of planning and think about how you want to approach this project. Each project in this book offers options for you to customize and make your own. Take some time to carefully choose the base fabric you want to embroider on, as it will set the tone of the piece from the start.

This project can be simplified to just the embroidery on a solid background. To give yourself a challenge and add dimension to the piece, you can use simple raw-edge appliqué (see page 86).

Threads & Stitches

Depending on the color of your base fabric, you may want to use the colors of thread suggested here, or you can choose different variations. I like to collect all of my threads and lay them on top of the fabric and next to each other to see if I like the effect. For each project, I tape a small bundle of thread tied in a knot to a piece of paper to keep track of the colors I'm using. It's a fun exercise, and if you need to buy more thread, it gives you a record of what you've used.

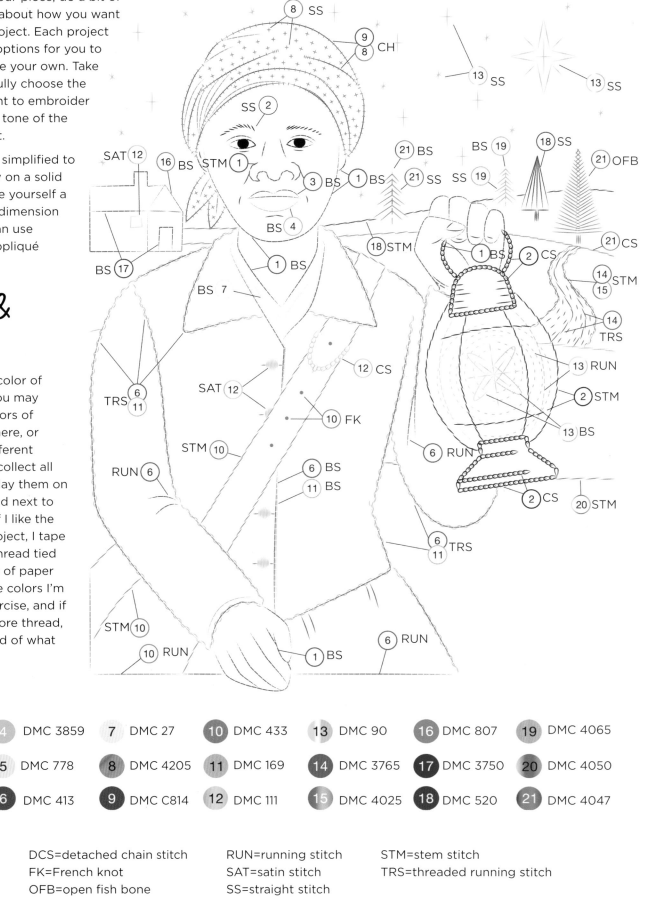

THREAD GUIDE

1 DMC 938	4 DMC 3859	7 DMC 27	10 DMC 433
2 DMC 310	5 DMC 778	8 DMC 4205	11 DMC 169
3 DMC 315	6 DMC 413	9 DMC C814	12 DMC 111

13 DMC 90	16 DMC 807	19 DMC 4065
14 DMC 3765	17 DMC 3750	20 DMC 4050
15 DMC 4025	18 DMC 520	21 DMC 4047

STITCHES USED

BS=backstitch
CH=couching
CS=chain stitch

DCS=detached chain stitch
FK=French knot
OFB=open fish bone

RUN=running stitch
SAT=satin stitch
SS=straight stitch

STM=stem stitch
TRS=threaded running stitch

Pattern

When transferring this design, if you are going to use the raw-edge appliqué method, make sure both images are the same size when you transfer them. When I embroidered my appliqué piece, the only area where I transferred the pattern to fabric was the face. I used the fabric shapes as a guide. If you are not doing the appliqué, transfer the whole design or modify with your drawings as you like.

Fabric Appliqué Option

Remember that this step is completely optional! I've included this portrait with an added layer to demonstrate to you how adaptable and customizable these projects are. If you want to take the time on this or any of the portraits to add an interesting background, fabric collage is a great technique to use. You can layer the stitching right on top of the collaged fabric pieces. You can use as much or as little fabric collage as you want; for example, you could just use appliqué in your portrait of Harriet to enhance her image.

The technique I've used is called raw-edge appliqué. With this technique, you don't need to worry about seam allowances (inlays) or clipping points, and you can choose to stitch around the shapes or not. With a bit of adaptation, you can use the same embroidery steps on fabric collage as you would on a solid background. I've used fabric from the stash in my studio and found some really great batiks and blenders that give the appearance of a solid color but with a bit of texture, allowing the embroidery to stand out. If you choose not to do the fabric appliqué, skip this altogether and get to stitching.

The numbers on this image indicate the individual pieces of fabric appliqué. Use these when tracing and cutting out the shapes in the image (see page 87).

The dashed lines indicate areas of fabric overlap.

Gathering Materials for Appliqué

There are quite a few methods for making a raw-edge appliqué, so feel free to research the method you like best. I've used a double-stick fusible web called Lite Steam-a-Seam 2®. Here are the materials you'll need:

- Lite Steam-a-Seam 2
- Fineline water-resistant marker
- Iron and ironing surface
- Nonstick pressing sheet (optional but nice to have)
- Quilting cotton or lightweight linen in a variety of colors and textured prints
- Tracing or tissue paper
- All-purpose scissors

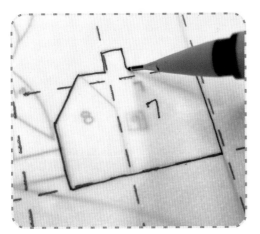

STEP 1: TRACE SHAPES
When using double-stick fusible web, you'll need to make sure you trace the reverse of the shapes.

STEP 2: CUT SHAPES
Create a bit of margin (¼" is plenty) around the shapes when you cut them out. This will allow the shapes to be fully covered in the final cut.

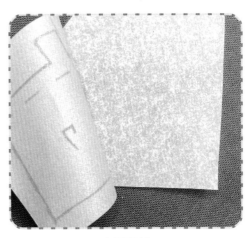

STEP 3: PEEL BACKING
Remove the backing from the cut piece to reveal a sticky adhesive.

STEP 4: STICK AND IRON
Finger press or lightly iron the shapes onto the wrong (back) side of the fabric.

STEP 5: CUT FINAL SHAPES
Cut the shape out on the drawn line. Remember you can always cut off more if you cut this shape too large.

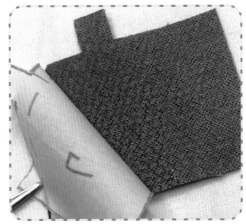

STEP 6: PEEL BACKING AGAIN
Peel off the backing. This is the side with the adhesive that you will stick down to your base fabric. Repeat this process for each piece of fabric appliqué.

STEP 7A: PLACEMENT
To place the appliqué pieces properly, trace the black-and-white line drawing on a piece of tissue paper. Tape it at the top and reposition the pieces as needed, checking as you go.

STEP 7B: LAYERING
Layer the background appliqué pieces, layering other pieces on top. You want to embroider the eyes and mouth, as they are tiny pieces to appliqué.

STEP 8: FINAL IRON
When all the pieces are stuck in place, press them down firmly and give the piece a final iron according to the directions on the fusible package.

Embroidering the Appliqué

Whew! Now it's time to embroider! The embroidery steps will be almost the same whether or not you choose to appliqué. You will just need to adjust some things as you go, adding more or less thread details. Take the house, for example. You may choose not to embroider it at all and just leave the fabric appliqué as it is, keeping it simple, or you may choose to stitch the outline details.

TIP

Use tweezers to help manage small pieces of fabric.

Face & Head Wrap

I've kept the basic structure of Harriet Tubman's face fairly simple. Feel free to go back in and add more details, shadows, or highlights if you'd like, or change the color and pattern on the head wrap. I've used a thicker yarn for the couching on the head wrap to give it a bit more texture. You could redraw this and either stitch her hair or add a different hat after doing some photographic research into her outfits and accessories.

STEP 1
Using backstitch, embroider the outlines of the face, including the upper eyelids. Use stem stitches to embroider the nose, shortening them around small curves. Use small straight stitches for details like the creases by the mouth and eyes. You can also use stem stitches for all of the details if you like.

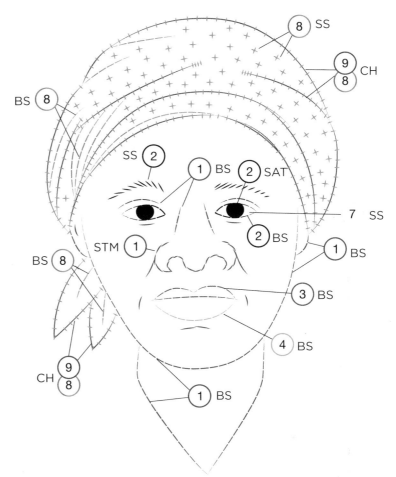

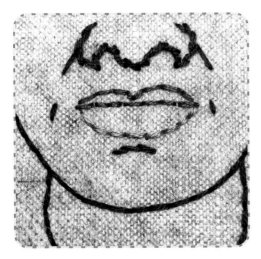

STEP 2
Outline the lips using maroon and medium pink. Adjust the size of the backstitches as you maneuver around the corners and creases.

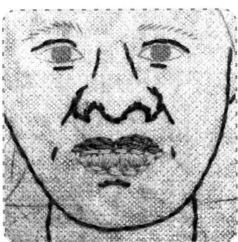

STEP 3
Fill the upper and lower lips with two shades of maroon and pink using different sizes of straight stitches. Overlap the stitches as needed, changing direction to show dimension.

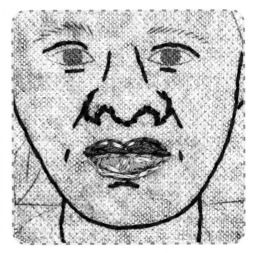

STEP 4
Add highlight stitches using a light-pink color. Using two strands of the darkest brown, add straight stitches to give a bit of definition between the lips and add a tiny bit of shadow around the edges.

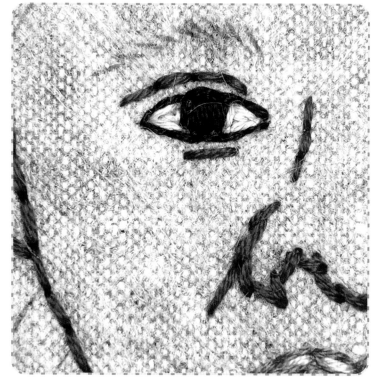

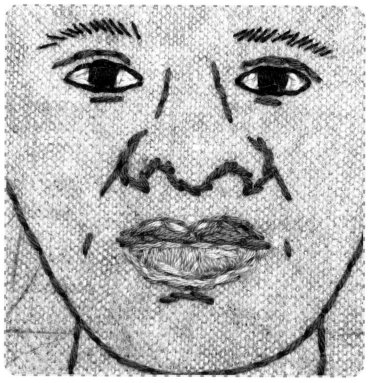

STEP 5
Using two strands, fill in the iris and pupil shape with satin stitch. Outline the top and bottom eyelids with black thread and backstitch. Using two strands and straight stitches, fill in the whites of the eyes.

STEP 6
Stitch the eyebrows with one strand of black thread. You can use two here if you'd like, but I like using one to keep it more delicate.

STEP 7
Using a darker, thicker thread, outline the head wrap with couching stitch. Add the wrinkle details in the head wrap using backstitch.

STEP 8
Add the pattern in the head wrap using a single strand of straight stitch (or cross stitch).

Jacket, Bag & Hands

I've kept the jacket and bag details fairly simple, but you could continue to add more details or even change the outfit that Harriet Tubman is wearing, including the styling and color. I like using the threaded running stitch to outline the jacket, as it adds dimension and a bit of color variation. You may want to add sparkle to the buckle and buttons using a metallic thread. I've chosen a blue linen to embroider on to represent a nighttime scene. Be mindful of the colors of thread you are using and how they interact with the base fabric to create a mood.

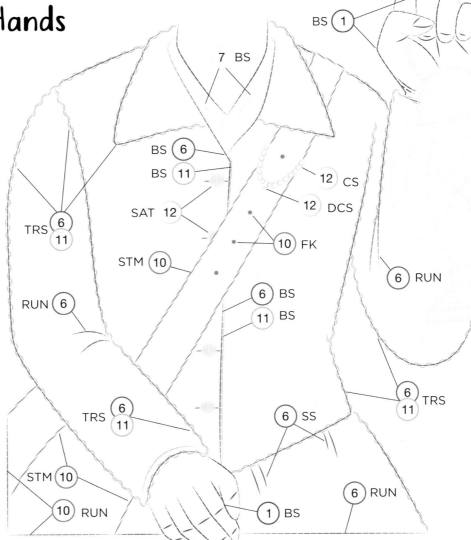

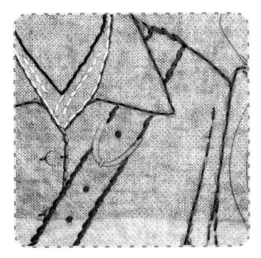

STEP 1
Outline the jacket using threaded running stitch. This will give the outline a bit of weight and texture. Add backstitch for the creases in the jacket. Using backstitch, add the white shirt. Stitch the bag strap with six strands of thread and stem stitch.

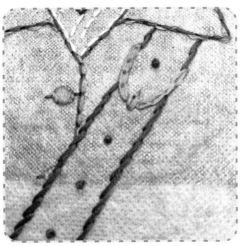

STEP 2
Using satin stitch, embroider the buttons. Chain stitches add nice dimension to the buckle. With French knots, indicate the holes in the strap. Use metallic thread here for some sparkle!

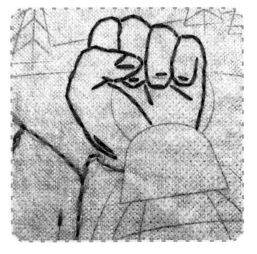

STEP 3
Embroider the hands using backstitch and straight stitches as needed to add details to the fingers.

lantern

Start by embroidering the light inside the lantern first, creating a soft glow using one strand of thread for the larger circles around the center light. Then proceed to stitch the other parts of the lantern on top of the light. Feel free to change up the shape of the lantern.

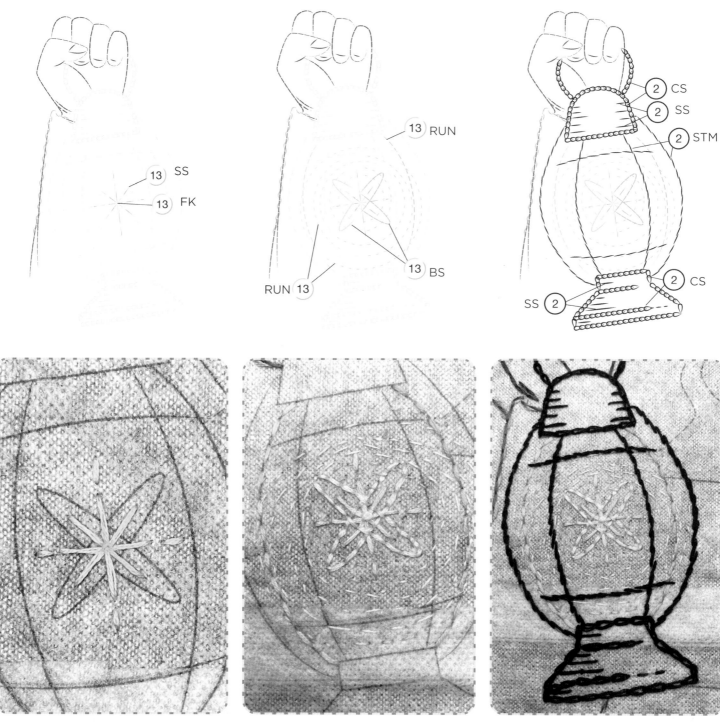

STEP 1
Create the central "star" of the light source using straight stitches.

STEP 2
Building up the layers of light, stitch the elongated ovals using backstitch. Create the radiating light using one strand of thread with running stitches in concentric circles. Stitch the outsides of the glass with three strands and running stitch.

STEP 3
Stitch the base and top of the lantern using chain stitch for added texture. Straight stitches add a bit of dimension. Outline the cage of the lantern using stem stitches, which are great for creating curves.

Background

We're almost there! Harriet Tubman utilized not only her intellect to escape slavery and guide others to freedom, but the rivers and stars helped guide her as well.

The background of your portrait can be as detailed or simple as you'd like. I like to add lots of details, just because that's my style. Once I've added the stitches below, I wash off the water-soluble stabilizer and add more stitches to fill in areas. Again, make this your own by redesigning the trees or the river!

STEP 1
Stitch the outline of the house using backstitch. Fill the window with satin stitch. Using light blue and satin stitch, stitch the front of the house.

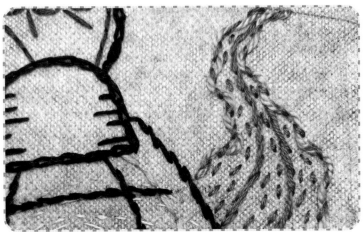

STEP 2
Outline the river using a threaded running stitch. Using a perle cotton adds a nice bit of texture here. Fill the river with stem stitches and seed stitches (which are basically tiny straight stitches!).

STEP 3

I've used different stitches and shades of green to add interest and texture to the trees. Practice on a scrap piece of fabric before stitching your portrait.

STEP 4

Stitch the North Star using straight stitches. For the main star, I've used six strands, with three strands for the secondary details and one strand for fine details. Stitch the starry sky using straight stitches in cross and star shapes.

This is what the appliqué base looks like without the embroidery. After building this fabric appliqué base, you can then embroider on top using the instructions in this project.

First, wash away the water-soluble stabilizer. If you're using this to transfer your pattern, you'll be able to see more clearly where you want to add stitches and details. After removing the white stabilizer, I've used a darker denim-colored linen to show the contrast of the stitches on the darker fabric and give a different perspective. I've added more details to the grassy areas and Harriet's name too.

RUTH BADER GINSBURG

RUTH BADER GINSBURG, aka RBG or "the Notorious RBG," was the second female justice to be appointed to the United States Supreme Court. From an early age, Ruth dreamed of becoming a lawyer and representing clients in the pursuit of justice. She advocated for gender equality and women's rights and was known for expressing her femininity and sense of style through her extensive collection of collars. Each one had political and personal meaning and symbolized her strong feminist legacy. Ruth Bader Ginsburg's fiery dissents catapulted her into an unexpected American icon. She died at age 87 on September 18, 2020, from complications from cancer. Upon hearing of her death, the country mourned her loss. She continues to inspire after her death and her words and contributions to the country remain.

Spend some time learning about RBG's life for ideas on embellishing your embroidery design. Look online for reference photos of her various collars and earrings and swap out the ones I've drawn if you like. Another idea is to embroider a quote onto her robe or background.

Suggestions include:

"Fight for the things that you care about, but do it in a way that will lead others to join you."

"My mother told me to be a lady. And for her, that meant be your own person, be independent."

"Women belong in all places where decisions are being made. It shouldn't be that women are the exception."

"I would like to be remembered as someone who used whatever talent she had to do her work to the very best of her ability."

Stitch & Color Guide

The Ruth Bader Ginsburg project is designed to be the most challenging in this book—but that doesn't mean you can't modify, simplify, or add to it! The technique I've used in the face is called "thread painting," and it is a fun, yet challenging, way to embroider. You can approach it as I've outlined it here and reference my final embroidery on page 111, or simplify it and just use outlines instead of fill stitches. Either way, have fun with it and take your time.

Threads & Stitches

You'll need quite a few colors to capture the different skin tones, build up the colors, and create depth in the face. I've used three strands of DMC threads in most of the design, except for the details in the eyes and mouth and the gemstones on RBG's collar, where I've used two strands for this star stitch. Variegated threads are a great way to add more color to your stitches, and I've used those for the lacy work. Her hair would be a great place to use this type of thread too. Finally, I've added some seed beads to the pattern around her head for a bit of sparkle.

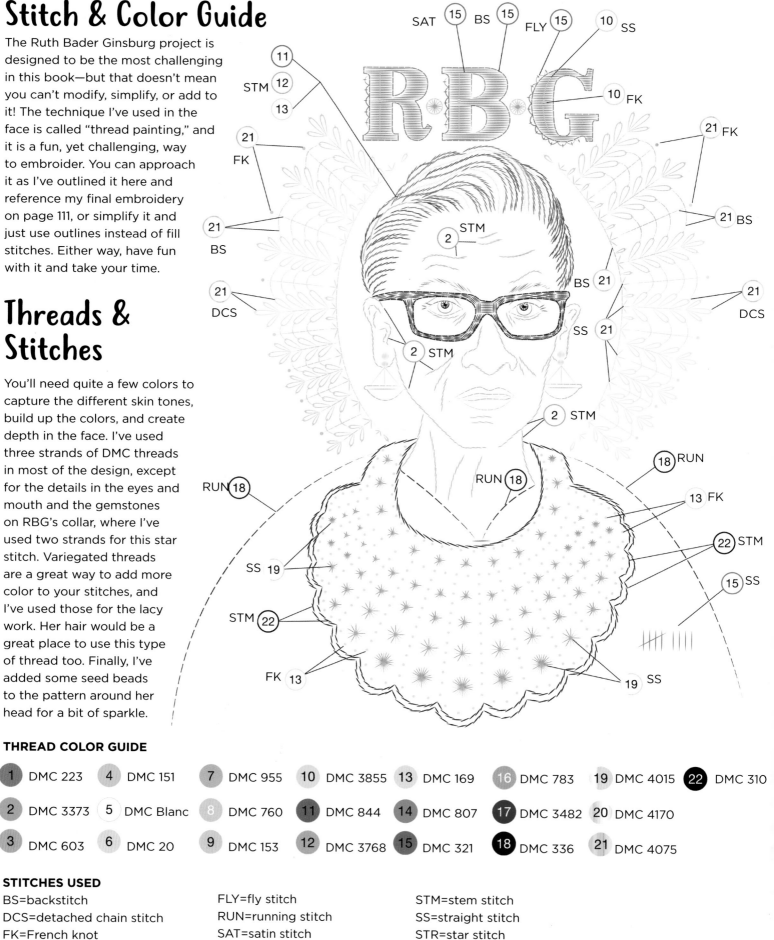

THREAD COLOR GUIDE

1 DMC 223	4 DMC 151	7 DMC 955	10 DMC 3855	13 DMC 169	16 DMC 783	19 DMC 4015	22 DMC 310
2 DMC 3373	5 DMC Blanc	8 DMC 760	11 DMC 844	14 DMC 807	17 DMC 3482	20 DMC 4170	
3 DMC 603	6 DMC 20	9 DMC 153	12 DMC 3768	15 DMC 321	18 DMC 336	21 DMC 4075	

STITCHES USED

BS=backstitch
DCS=detached chain stitch
FK=French knot

FLY=fly stitch
RUN=running stitch
SAT=satin stitch

STM=stem stitch
SS=straight stitch
STR=star stitch

Pattern

Because there is a lot of detail in this image, think about how large you want to make your design. The smaller it is, the more challenging it will be to stitch details into areas such as the face and gemstones on the collar. If you want to make the design smaller, consider redrawing the design and taking out some details. My original embroidery is 9" x 11" wide for reference. I printed the design onto two sheets of water-soluble stabilizer and pieced them together at this size.

Thread Painting

Painting or drawing with thread is similar to working with watercolor or gouache, as I do in my illustrations. However, instead of brushstrokes, you use stitches to create line and form. I'm mixing colors as I go, following the direction and movement of facial features. As you approach this embroidery, start first with the hair, outlining the features, and then work to fill in the larger areas with thread. By overlapping and layering different colors of thread, you'll create form, texture, and movement.

This is an intuitive process, so use this as a guide to stitching, and step back from your work often to take a break and view your work from a distance to gain perspective. Use this guide to stitch the overall effect of the face. Add longer stitches for bigger areas of color and shorten the stitches in detailed areas, such as the eyes, nose, mouth, and ears. Your stitches will look different from mine, and that's OK!

Hair

Start by stitching the hair. This will give context to the face and allow you to blend the area of the forehead that meets the hairline. Begin with the darkest color, then the medium gray, and finally add the highlights. You can add more dark or light color as needed when the hair is finished to capture the shadow and highlights. I've used three strands of thread, but you could certainly use six or a wool yarn to give the hair more texture.

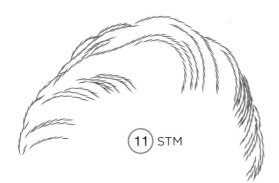

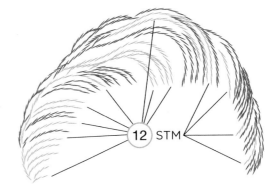

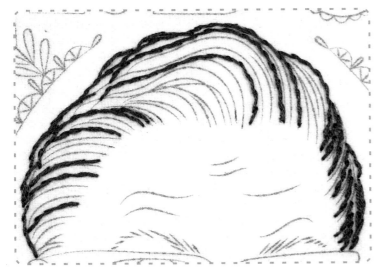

STEP 1
Stitch the darkest color using stem stitch. You can also work the hair in sections, as opposed to stitching each color separately.

STEP 2
Add the medium gray.

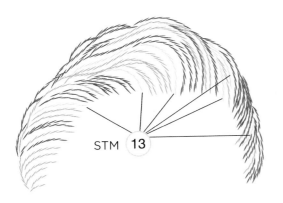

STEP 3
Add the lightest gray for the highlights; then step back and assess whether you want to fill in more darker or lighter areas.

Face & Neck Outlines

Again, think of embroidering the face like painting. Switch back and forth between colors of thread as you work through the different areas. Start with the outlines; then fill in the facial features. Afterward, go back and stitch the outlines again with a slightly darker color to add definition to the features. You can also just stitch the outlines and add minimal details—it's up to you! Use three strands of thread for the outlines.

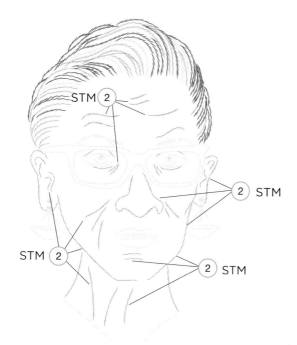

STEP 1

Outline the features of the face using a stem stitch. Adjust the stitch lengths as needed, making smaller stitches to go around tight curves.

STEP 2

Stitch the light gray of the eyebrows using straight stitches of varied lengths. Add dark gray details on top.

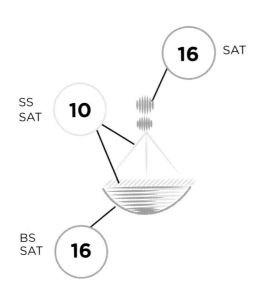

STEP 3
Add earrings that look like the scales of justice! First stitch the circles on the earlobes using satin stitch. Add three long straight stitches to form a triangle and satin stitch the highlights of the bottom of the scale. Backstitch the outline and satin stitch fill the shadow.

ACCESSORIZE

Ruth Bader Ginsburg was known for accessorizing her black robes with various collars, all of which had a different meaning. Add visual interest to your portrait of RBG with any number of collars and accessories, including necklaces and earrings. Do an online search for the meaning behind her collars and pick your favorite!

Face & Neck Fill

This is where the fun really begins! Refer to the stitch map on page 100 as a guide to embroidering the face. It will require building up the stitches and, often, going back several times to add highlights or shadows. You can approach this by either stitching color by color, as I've outlined below, or by sections of the face, stitching multiple colors at the same time (right).

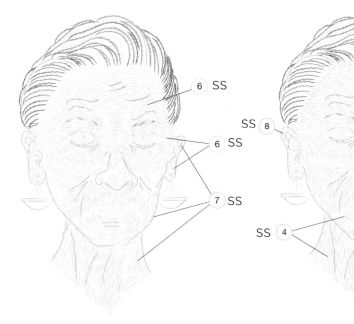

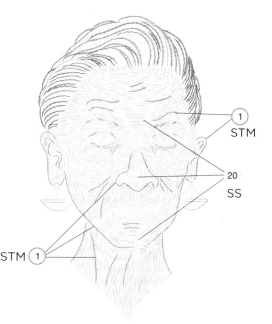

STEP 1

Start by stitching the main skin color and adding light green to begin the shadows. You're just building a base here and will blend in the other colors as you go. Pay attention to the direction of the stitches; this will help create texture, movement, and dimension.

STEP 2

At this stage, things may start to look "bad" before they look good, but keep going! Here you'll build the shadows and midtones of the skin using four more colors. Use the colors I've indicated, or feel free to choose brighter colors if you prefer!

STEP 3

Add highlights to give the nose and forehead more dimension. After the face is filled in, use a darker color to again outline the facial features to give them more definition. Use your judgment here; you might not need to stitch over every outline.

Glasses

This embroidery will really come to life when the glasses are added. The dark contrast gives the piece a lot of dimension, and the eyes and mouth give it personality! Be patient here; the eyes and mouth require small stitches to get the details right. You may find it helpful to use a thimble to push the needle through the fabric and layers of stitches more easily.

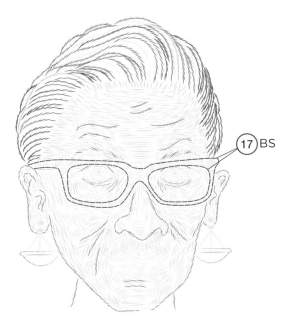

STEP 1
Outline the glasses in medium blue using backstitch.

STEP 2
Fill the glasses with medium blue, varying the direction of the stitch.

STEP 3
Add dark blue stitches to give the glasses a bit of dimension, placing the stitches on top of and between the stitches in the first layer of blue.

Eyes

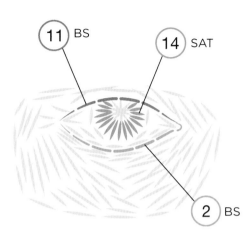

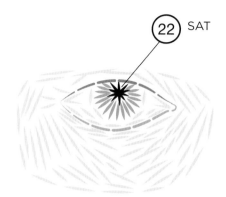

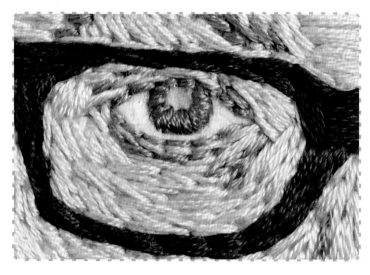

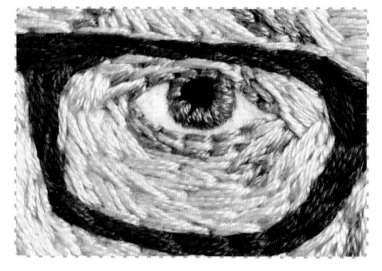

STEP 1

Stitch the iris with light blue using satin stitch, working from the center outward in a circle. Leave room in the center for the pupil. Stitch the top lid using medium gray and the bottom lid using a backstitch.

STEP 2

Stitch the pupil using tiny black satin stitches.

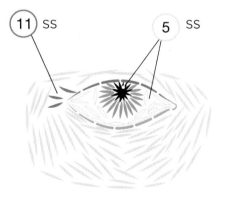

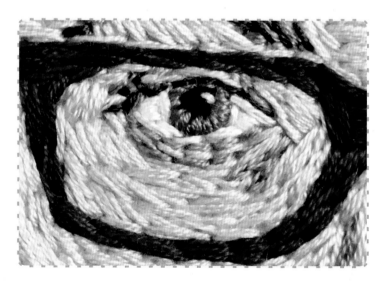

STEP 3

Add a highlight to the pupil using one or two tiny stitches. Add the whites of the eyes. Then, using small straight stitches, add three tiny eyelashes.

Mouth

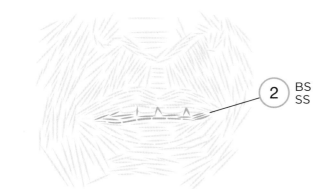

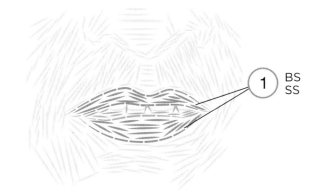

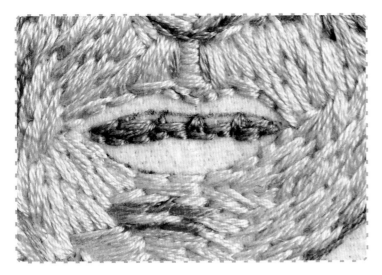

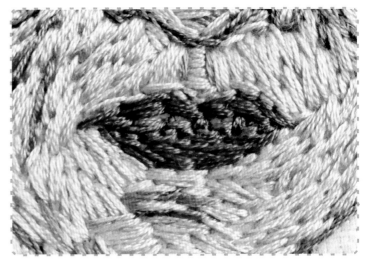

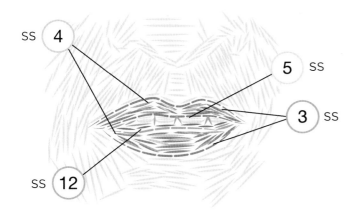

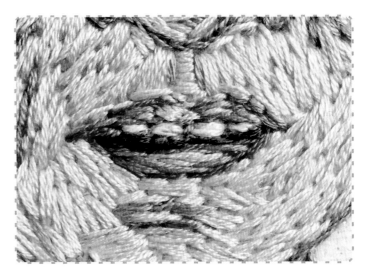

STEP 1
Stitch the inside of the mouth with a combination of backstitch and straight stitches. Use just enough to fill the area between the teeth and lips

STEP 2
Stitch the base color of the lips. It's OK if there are some gaps; you'll add highlights in the next step.

STEP 3
Add a medium pink tone to begin to build dimension in the lips. Then add light pink highlights and a few stitches for the teeth. Finally, create dark gray stitches for depth in the open area of the mouth.

lacework

The lacework around RBG's head is inspired by one of her collars. It consists of a few design elements repeated many times and is brought to life by a variegated thread. For a bit of sparkle, I've added seed beads in varying yellow colors after completing the embroidery. You could also use metallic gold thread for this area to make it extra special. The earrings representing the scales of justice could also be accented with metallic thread.

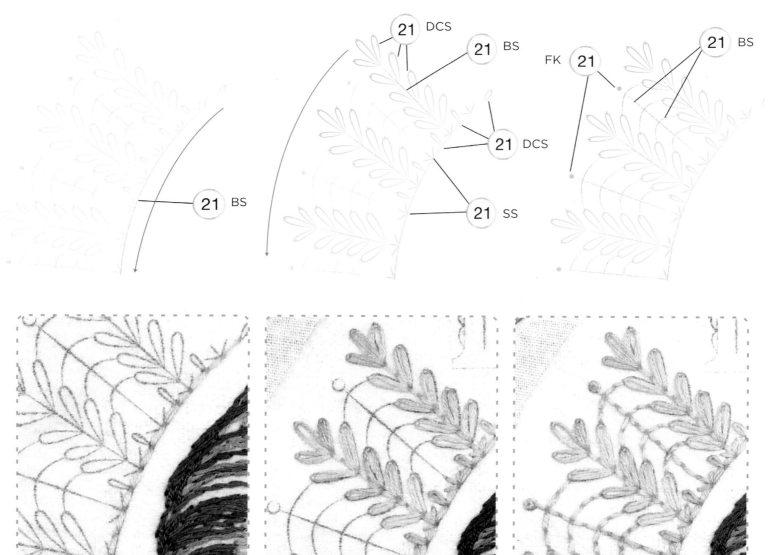

STEP 1
Stitch a curved line from top to bottom using the backstitch.

STEP 2
Return to the starting point and, working your way down the backstitched line, add the radiating lines, backstitch first, and then detached chain stitches. Add the details along the original line as you go. You'll find your stitching rhythm.

STEP 3
Add the remaining backstitched radiating lines with a French knot atop each one. Add yellow and gold seed beads at this point if you'd like more sparkle. Repeat these steps to fill in the lacework on the other side.

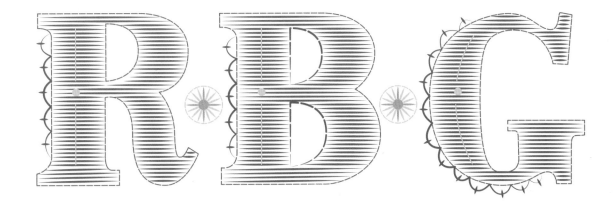

RBG Type

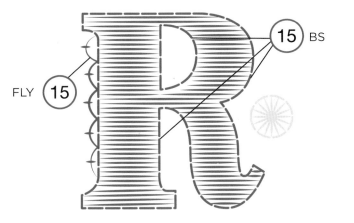

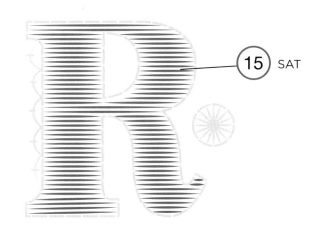

STEP 1

Fill the letters with satin stitch. Don't worry about lining up the edges perfectly; the backstitch you'll add next will cover up any rough edges.

STEP 2

Outline the letters with a backstitch. Add fly stitch around the edges of the letters to create a scalloped look.

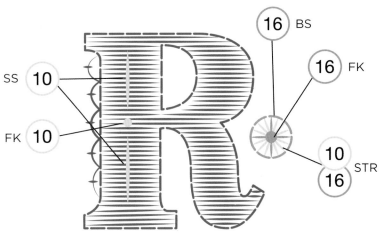

STEP 3

Add details with yellow on top of the satin stitch. To create the "stones" between the letters, make a star stitch in the center and outline with backstitch. Add a French knot in the center.

Collar & Robe

Justice Ginsburg wore this collar to give a dissenting opinion. It looks more complicated than it is; really, it's just a lot of star stitches in different sizes, with French knots outlined by slip stitches.

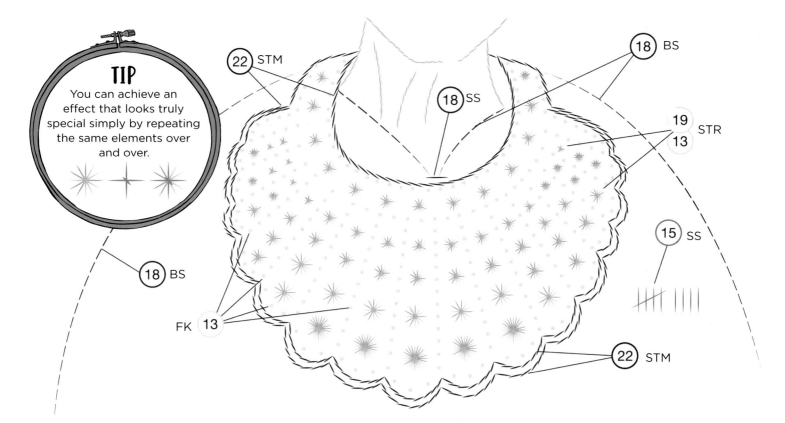

TIP
You can achieve an effect that looks truly special simply by repeating the same elements over and over.

STEP 1
Outline the black edges of the collar using stem stitch; then outline the edges of the robe with dark blue. You can keep this simple, or, as I've done, fill it with varying sizes of running stitches in a lighter blue.

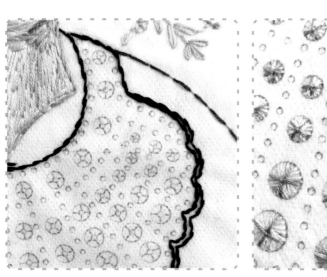

STEP 2
Add the "gemstones" to the collar. There are a few different sizes here; you'll use fewer stitches in the smaller stones. Start with one long straight stitch; then add the other straight stitches in a radiating circle. This will give dimension to the stone. Switch to solid gray and add two long stitches on top to form a cross and one small stitch to lock them down.

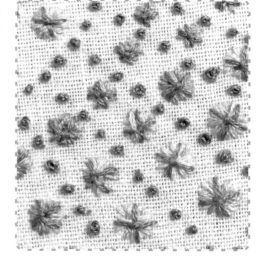

STEP 3
Finally, add the French knots. These represent small gemstones on the collar.

Add nine red stitches to the robe to represent Justice Ginsburg famously saying that there will be enough women on the U.S. Supreme Court only when there are nine.

MICHELLE OBAMA

When They Go Low, We GO HIGH —mo

MICHELLE OBAMA is inspirational on so many levels. One of the great things about Michelle Obama is the diversity of time periods in her life to research and learn about, from her childhood on the South Side of Chicago and her time at Princeton and Harvard universities to her position as First Lady of the United States. She is inspirational on so many levels! As FLOTUS, she aimed to reduce childhood obesity and encourage a healthy lifestyle in children, motivate students to continue their education past high school, and address the challenges that keep girls from receiving an education. She has gone on to become a best-selling author and continues to fight for diversity and gender equality across numerous industries.

Here are some quotes from Michelle Obama that you might consider embroidering:

"When someone is cruel or acts like a bully, you don't stoop to their level. No, our motto is, 'When they go low, we go high.'"

"Your story is what you have, what you will always have. It is something to own."

"Don't be afraid. Be focused. Be determined. Be hopeful. Be empowered."

"Choose people who lift you up."

CHOOSE PEOPLE WHO LIFT YOU UP

Stitch & Color Guide

You can really have fun with this project by using different threads and yarns to stitch the type. If you have wool threads or sparkly yarns on hand, try using those to add some interest. Instead of using the stem stitch for the type, try couching with a chunky yarn. I used a pretty mauve-colored linen, so be playful with the fabric you chose too!

Threads & Stitches

Gather the threads you'll need and decide how you want to approach this design. I've used mostly DMC six-strand thread divided into three strands, but I've also mixed in size 5 cotton perle. DMC's thread colors are generally interchangeable, so a blue #798 is the same in cotton perle as it is for the six-strand.

THREAD GUIDE

1 DMC 433	**4** DMC 4140	**7** DMC 310	**10** DMC 152	**13** DMC 4075	**16** DMC 798	**19** DMC 351
2 DMC 3031	**5** DMC Blanc	**8** DMC 223	**11** DMC 315	**14** DMC C444	**17** DMC 336	
3 DMC 3371	**6** DMC 317	**9** DMC 3688	**12** MET GOLD	**15** DMC 3766	**18** DMC 722	

STITCHES USED

BS=backstitch
CH=couching

FK=French knot
RUN=running stitch

SAT=satin stitch
SS=straight stitch

STM=stem stitch

Pattern

Use your method of choice to transfer this design to the fabric. Keep as many details as you like, or add others based on your own research. If you want to stitch a different quote, sketch it out first to get the placement correct.

Face

When embroidering the face in this project, try to make each stitch as efficient as possible. Don't fuss over the stitches too much, and don't overstitch an area. If you're unsure how to stitch the mouth or eyes, take a few minutes and practice on a scrap of fabric...and then go for it! Remember that the eyes and mouth are a small part of the overall portrait, so keep the stitching simple.

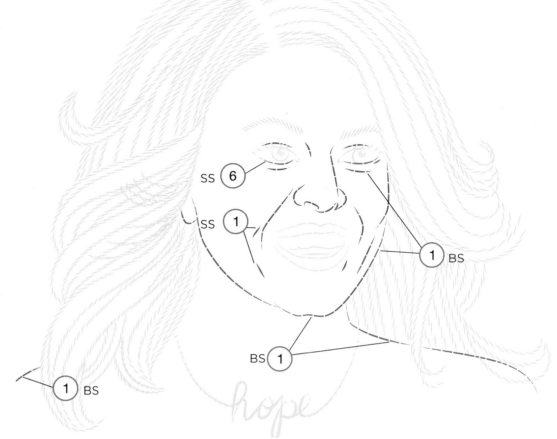

STEP 1

Using backstitch, embroider the outlines of the face including the nose. Use smaller stitches to navigate around the tight corners of the nostrils. Use small straight stitches for details like the creases by the mouth.

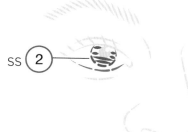

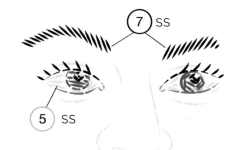

STEP 2

Outline the iris with backstitch and fill the area with small straight stitches. Leave room for the black pupil.

STEP 3

Add black straight stitches for the pupils and backstitch for the upper eyelids. Add small straight stitches for the eyelashes and the inner corners of the eyes.

STEP 4

Add small straight stitches to indicate the whites of the eyes. Using two strands of white thread, add a few tiny stitches as highlights on the pupils. Stitch the eyebrows using straight stitches.

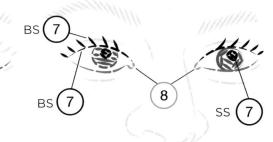
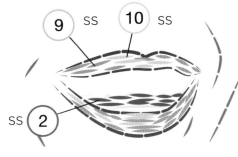
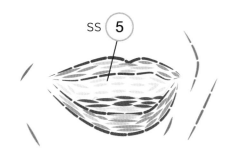

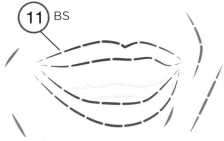

STEP 5

Outline the lips using a dark mauve or dusty pink color. I've mixed in a few straight stitches on the corners of the mouth.

STEP 6

Fill the upper and lower lips with two shades of the pink using different sizes of straight stitches. Overlap them as needed, but keep them simple. Add darker straight stitches for the area between the teeth.

STEP 7

Add small straight stitches for the teeth. You can also simplify the teeth further and use just a few longer stitches on the upper and lower teeth.

Hair

When stitching the hair, the idea is to create highlights and shadows to indicate volume. I've used variegated thread to get lots of color in the medium tones. Fill in the hair as much as you want, adding more lines if you'd like. You can also research different hairstyles that Michelle Obama has worn over the years and change it up!

STEP 1

Stitch light-colored strands of hair using a variegated thread and stem stitches.

STEP 2

Layer in the light brown color using stem stitch. Use smaller stitches in the tighter curves of the hair.

STEP 3

Continue to build volume with medium and dark thread colors. Add more strands if you want to fill in the empty areas at this stage.

STEP 4

Using the variegated color, stitch the wisps of hair on top of the existing stitches.

Necklace & Sweater

As you stitch the necklace and sweater, look through your stash of yarns and threads to see if you have something fuzzy or metallic that could add more dimension. A wool thread would be fun for the sweater. Change the color if you wish!

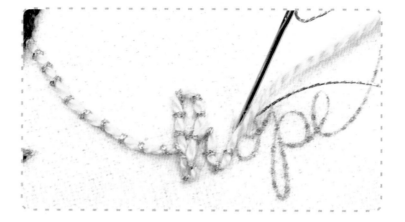

STEP 1

Using perle cotton and metallic gold threads, lay down the perle and stitch it in place with metallic gold. Place stitches closer together to form the tight curves of the letters.

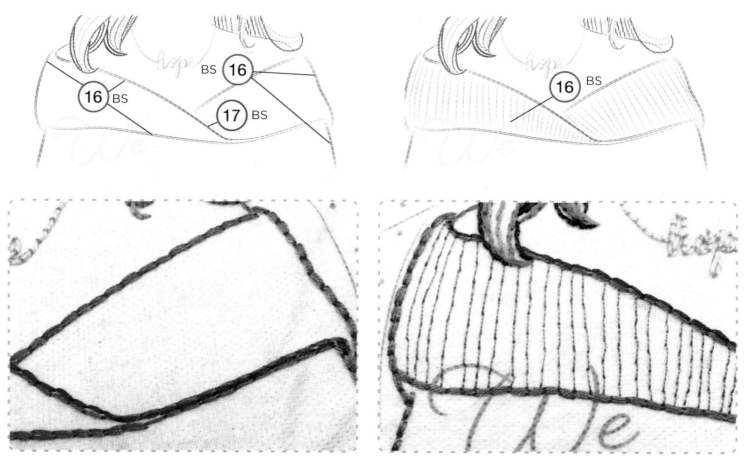

STEP 2

Outline the sweater using two lines of backstitch. Add one line of dark blue using backstitch to indicate a shadow.

STEP 3

If you'd like to add an extra detail to give the sweater more dimension, backstitch the "ribbing" using a single strand of thread. You can draw these lines first or just stitch them freehand. Chain stitch would make a fun alternative to backstitch here!

Typography

Sketch out your favorite quotes from Michelle Obama before adding them to your portrait. Stitches that work well for embroidering type include backstitch, chain stitch, and couching.

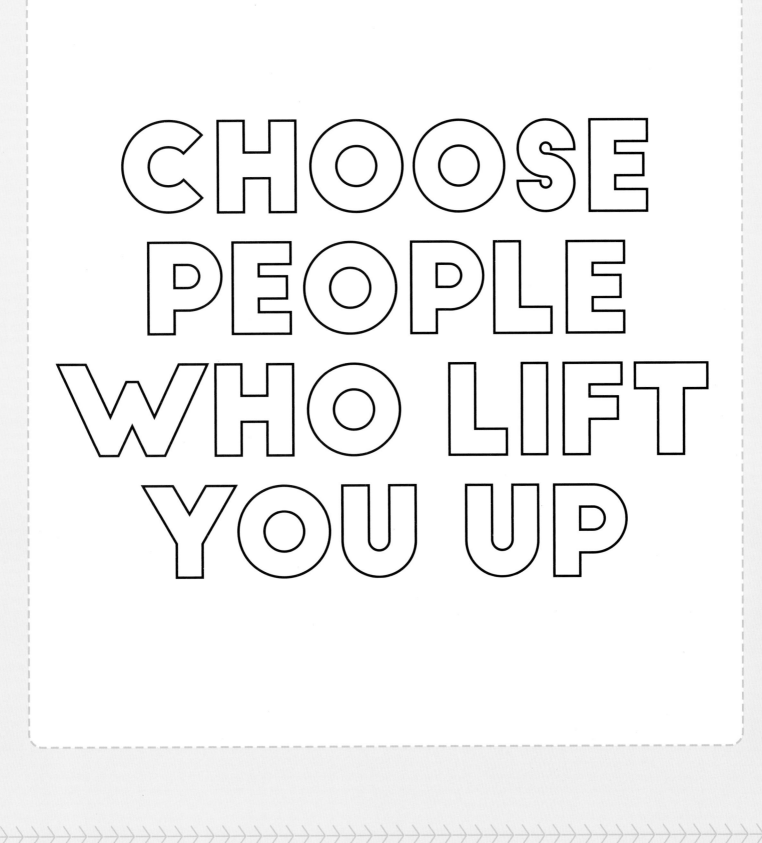

Type

This is where you can really have some fun with stitches and trying different types of yarn. When stitching the script type, if the yarn is too thick, the words may become less legible. When adding the final details, feel free to add more French knots or some seed stitches for more texture.

SS (13)
FK (13)
STM (17)

16 BS

BS (15)
SS (15)

STEP 1

Outline the banner with backstitch and fill the ends with satin stitch.

STEP 2

Using perle cotton, stitch the letters using stem stitch. Use smaller stitches to stitch around the tight corners and small details.

STEP 3

Add the final details to the radiating lines around the type. Feel free to add more embellishments if you'd like.

STM (17)

(17) RUN   (16) RUN   (14) RUN

SS (13)   (13) SS

We GO HIGH
—mo

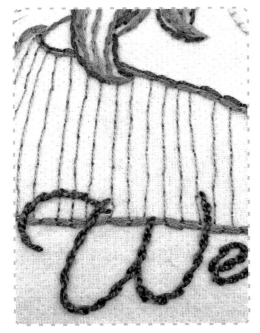

STEP 4

Using perle cotton, stem stitch the type using smaller stitches around the tight corners.

STEP 5

Use the running stitch to outline the block letters. Start with the dark blue line on the outside; then move to the yellow line inside; and finally, add the medium blue. I've used a cotton floss with a metallic sparkle for the yellow.

STEP 6

Add the decorative details using straight stitches. Use small backstitches to outline the sign off "—mo." Michelle Obama often included this when she wrote her own social media posts as FLOTUS.

Final Details

This last bit will make this embroidery really fun and add a pop of color. Add more of your own embellishments, or stitch some sketches if you like. Step back from your embroidery and enjoy the work you've done!

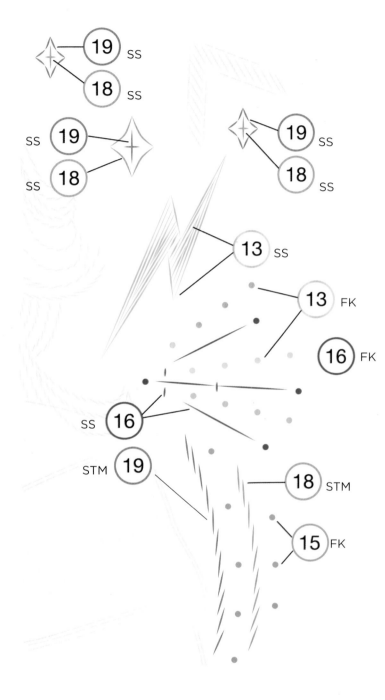

RESOURCES

Every embroiderer has their favorite needles, threads, fabrics, and other notions. There are so many sources for materials, including estate sales, yard sales, online, and friends cleaning out their studio stashes. Here are some of the materials and resources that I use daily for my work. I try to find what I'm looking for locally at small fabric shops, but sometimes I will order online or go to big-box stores. The key is to experiment with different tools and materials and discover what works for you.

Needles & Other Tools

- www.merchantandmills.com
- www.dritz.com
- www.dmc.com
- www.jjneedles.com
- en.tulip-japan.co.jp
- www.joann.com
- www.michaels.com
- www.123stitch.com
- Q-Snap™ embroidery frame: www.yarntree.com
- Wooden hoop stand: www.hawthornhandmade.com

Thread & Floss

- www.dmc.com
- www.lecien.co.jp/en
- www.purlsoho.com
- www.kreinik.com
- www.etsy.com
- www.ebay.com

I like to stitch on linen fabric with a lightweight cotton or linen backing. You will likely need to experiment with this to find what you like to use and what combination of fabric and backing you prefer. You can find nice-quality linens at local fabric stores or any of the following:

- www.boltfabricboutique.com
- www.fabricdepot.com
- www.moderndomesticpdx.com

Fabric & Fabric Appliqué

Lite EZ-Steam® II: www.pellonprojects.com and www.warmcompany.com

Dritz® Non-Stick Pressing Sheet (18" x 18"): www.joann.com

Transfer Materials

Water-soluble stabilizer: www.sulky.com

Stick-N-Washaway™: www.pellonprojects.com

Pilot® FriXion ColorSticks or FriXion Ball Clicker: www.pilotpen.us

Fine Point Mark-Be-Gone Marking Pen: www.dritz.com and www.joann.com

Artograph® LightPad® 930: www.artograph.com and www.dickblick.com

Fine Tip Iron-On Transfer Pen: www.sublimestitching.com

Iron-On Transfer Pen: Sulky.com

Aunt Martha Hot Iron Transfer Pencil: www.joann.com and other craft stores

Nonce® White Marking Pencil (water-soluble for transferring to dark fabrics): www.joann.com and other craft stores

TIP
Look for locally hand-dyed threads at craft stores and estate sales!

Drawing Materials

Saral® Wax Free Transfer Paper: www.jerrysartarama.com and www.dickblick.com

Copic® Multiliner Pen or Sakura® Pigma Micron Pen: www.dickblick.com and artistcraftsman.com

Canson® Tracing Paper (Foundation series): www.dickblick.com and artistcraftsman.com

Borden & Riley® Paris Bleedproof Paper For Pens: www.dickblick.com

About the Artist

Amy L. Frazer is an illustrator and embroiderer living and working among the plants and trees of Portland, Oregon. She is a multidisciplined craftsperson and a lover of all things made by hand. Through her work, she captures the beauty of the world around us and embellishes it with personal mark making. Amy believes that embroidery is a means to bring people together and build community and connections where previously none existed.

With a BFA from the Columbus College of Art & Design, Amy has a solid background in drawing and illustration and continues to take workshops and classes to hone her skills, stay fresh, and learn new techniques. She is a self-taught embroiderer and has taught workshops with local colleges and arts and nature organizations. With extensive experience in product creation from working at companies such as Galerie au Chocolat, Old Navy®, and Nike®, Amy enjoys designing objects as well as the prints and colors that adorn them.

Amy loves to travel and always has a bag packed for her next adventure to the mountains, the sea, or a fun city to explore and gather inspiration. Always with a portable art studio in tow, she finds moments of quiet to draw or embroider whenever she can.

Her popular on-the-go workshop, Hike N' Stitch™ (@Hike_n_Stitch), is a favorite with local hikers and stitchers in Portland. Her artwork has been featured in the *UPPERCASE Encyclopedia of Inspiration, Stitch-illo*; on seed packets for the Hudson Valley Seed Company; and in the popular Portland Trail Blazers gameday poster and "Made by Her" series.

Amy's grandmother, Pearl, was a major influence on her love of art making. When she views others' art, Amy likes to think that maybe their granny taught them how to make things too.

Amy lives in Portland with her boyfriend, Matthew, and their two dogs, Seymour and Josephine, who often get up to eat at 4:30 am.

You can see more of her work at www.AmyLFrazer.com or on Instagram @AmyLFrazer.

ALSO AVAILABLE FROM WALTER FOSTER PUBLISHING

**Art Makers: Polymer Clay
for Beginners**
978-1-63322-632-6

**Art Makers:
Papier-Mache**
978-1-63322-892-4

Visit www.QuartoKnows.com